Mindset of Faith

A Training Manual to Renew Your Mind and Walk in God-Consciousness

Written and Published by

Anita Newson (Page)

Copyright © 2025 by **Anita Newson**

All rights reserved.

Published in the United States by Anita Newson.

An imprint of A New Page Publishing House.

No part of this book may be reproduced, stored in a retrieval system, or transmitted in any form or by any means-electronic, mechanical, photocopying, recording, or otherwise without prior written permission from the author or publisher, except for brief quotations used in reviews or educational content.

ISBN: 979-8-9929169-0-4

Printed in the United States of America

Dedication

To my mother, **Annie Page** —Your unwavering love, prayers, and support have been the foundation of my strength. Thank you for being my greatest cheerleader and covering me in faith every step of the way.

To my sons — **Azaius Page, Lawrence Newson III, Nathan Newson, and Jacoby Newson** —You are my heart, my inspiration, and my most loyal fan base. Everything I do is with you in mind and for the legacy I pray you continue to carry with power and purpose.

And to everyone who has supported the call and assignment God placed on my life —Your encouragement, prayers, and belief in this work mean more than words can express. May God's blessings continue to overflow in your lives.

Acknowledgments

Apostle Zoe Legette

You have been a true inspiration and a foundational part of my spiritual journey. Because of your willingness to pour out and teach me about my identity in Christ, I now walk confidently in who I am and in the assignment God has given me. I love and appreciate the incredible Gift of God that you are.

Apostle Alberto De Leon

Your revelatory teaching and deep insight brought confirmation and clarity to this work. Because of the faithfulness and obedience that your life encompasses, it has left a lasting impact on my life and calling. The life work that you share is invaluable, and I am truly thankful to you.

Dr. Tracy Timberlake

Your guidance during the early stages of my entrepreneurial journey has been nothing short of life-changing. You've played a pivotal role in every stage of my growth, and I am deeply thankful for your wisdom, support, and belief in what God has called me to do.

Dr. Kristen Guillory

You have helped me step boldly into my God-given destiny. Your encouragement to embrace authenticity and move beyond my comfort zone has shifted the trajectory of my life and calling. Thank you for helping me fully show up as the woman God created me to be.

LaChelle Adkins

I am deeply thankful for your unwavering guidance, patience, and loyalty. As a trusted collaboration partner, cherished friend, and Sister in Christ, you have been an invaluable part of this journey. Your consistent support has meant more than words can express, and I am truly grateful for the role you continue to play in both my life and my calling.

Michelle Fuqua

Thank you for always being present, supportive, and responsive. Your generous heart and consistent encouragement throughout this process have not gone unnoticed. I am sincerely grateful to you and all you've contributed behind the scenes.

Amy Bearden

I appreciate your faith in this life work for me. Your encouragement and help are valued, and I love the person that you are and share with the world—***never change.***

Foreword

Dr. Tracy Timberlake
Multi-Award Winning (Faith-Based) Business Coach, Mindset Coach, Online Influencer, and Co-Founder of Flourish Media

In my line of work I get to interact with a myriad of different people. Many can talk the talk, but walking the walk is a different story. It is a rare privilege to witness someone walk so boldly in their God-given purpose really and truly. I have had the honor of coaching, working with and witnessing Anita for five years, and in that time, one thing has always been abundantly clear: her passion for helping others. Whether in life or business, Anita moves with a heart of service and a deep desire to see people walk in the fullness of their faith.

Her journey, as outlined in *Mindset of Faith*, is a powerful testament to what it means to trust God completely, even when the path is unclear. She has lived out the principles she now shares, and that authenticity shines through every page of this book. Anita does not merely teach faith - she embodies it from her own experiences and in her everyday life. She understands what it means to wrestle with doubt, to press through challenges, and to emerge stronger, wiser, and more anchored in God's promises.

What I love most about Anita's approach is that she doesn't just encourage you to believe - she equips you to apply. This book is more than a collection of motivational/inspirational words; it is a training ground for transformation. Through her personal experiences, biblical insights, and practical exercises, she invites us to shift your mindset, align with God's truth, and step boldly into the life He has called you to live.

If you've ever struggled with uncertainty, if you've ever questioned whether you are capable of stepping into God's best for you, then you are holding exactly what you need in your hands. Anita's words will challenge you, stretch you, and most importantly, remind you that faith is not passive; it is an active, living force that can move mountains!

May this work ignite something in you, as it has in me, and may you walk forward with a renewed *Mindset of Faith*.

Foreword

Zondra Evans
Media Entrepreneur, Speaker, Author, and Executive Producer and Founder of Zondra TV Network (ZTV)

There are moments in life when we encounter a work so steeped in truth and authenticity that it doesn't feel like mere reading—it feels like a divine encounter. Mindset of Faith is one of those rare works. More than just a book, it is a sacred guide, a powerful testimony, and a practical training manual for anyone ready to go deeper in their journey with God.

From the very first page, Anita's vulnerability, boldness, and unwavering trust in God shines through. Her faith walk—a journey marked by revelation and restoration—is a beautiful reminder that God's calling never expires, even when we are not sure of our next step.

This book will not only inspire you to believe in God—it will challenge you to live in God. It invites you to release limiting beliefs, reframe your thoughts, and embrace a mindset fueled by faith rather than fear. Each chapter is crafted to renew your mind and awaken your spirit.

If you're ready to be transformed—if you're ready to walk confidently in the identity God has placed within you—then what you need is this blueprint for divine alignment.

Prepare your heart. Let your faith rise. And allow the Holy Spirit to do what only He can: lead you into the fullness of who you were always meant to be.

Foreword

Alberto De Leon
Apostolic Overseer
Glory Mind Institute Basilea

Life can be lived at The Next Level, but only if we take the time to learn how to get there. Aspiring mountain climbers may have a strong desire to scale the highest peaks, but desire alone is not enough. Without the guidance of someone who has already navigated the treacherous paths, the summit remains out of reach.

In the natural world, Sherpas are renowned for their intimate knowledge of mountainous terrains, particularly the formidable peaks of the Himalayas. They are indigenous to the region, having lived their lives in the very environment that others seek to conquer. They understand not only the visible landscape but also the hidden challenges — the shifting weather, the fragile paths, the subtle signs of danger. It is through their wisdom, endurance, and insight that many climbers are able to reach heights they could never achieve on their own.

Similarly, in the spiritual realm, we need guides who have lived in the heights of faith — those who understand its terrain, its challenges, and its unseen currents. Anita is such a guide. She has lived within the locus of faith, having not only studied, but embodying the mindset and the life that faith demands. As a Native, she understands the spiritual environment — its demands, its disciplines, and its great rewards — and she knows the equipment necessary to scale its highest elevations: the Word of God, the discipline of belief, and most importantly, the practice of walking in God's love.

While it is possible to ascend to certain levels of faith on your own, true spiritual mastery — the kind that not only transforms circumstances, but the very core of who you are — requires a guide. Anita's mission is not to lead you to material peaks such as new houses, cars, or earthly achievements [nothing wrong with any of those things]. However, her passion is to guide believers from the baseline of faith — simply believing the Word — to the summit of faith, which is walking fully and freely in the love of God as you incarnate His very Word.

Through her insights, teachings, and example, you will be equipped not merely to survive in faith, but to change and conquer. With Anita as your guide, you are invited to ascend beyond Moments of Faith into the extraordinary heights of the Mindset of Faith — the true summit of the Christian life.

Table of Contents

Introduction ---XVII

CHAPTER 1: What is Faith? ------------------------------------1

CHAPTER 2: The Power in Bold Faith --------------------30

CHAPTER 3: Faith IS a Mindset -----------------------------48

CHAPTER 4: Let's Sum It Up ---------------------------------65

CHAPTER 5: How the Brain and Mind Work Together ---70

CHAPTER 6: The Regenerated Mind(set) --------------866

CHAPTER 7: Faith Requires God-Consciousness ----100

CHAPTER 8: The Conclusion of the Matter is LOVE ---1146

CHAPTER 9: Putting it All Together -------------------121

CHAPTER 10: Declaring "IT IS SO" For You -----------127

GLOSSARY---133

REFERENCES--141

BIBLICAL TRANSLATIONS--------------------------------143

AUTHOR BIOGRAPHY---------------------------------------150

INTRODUCTION

"But I have prayed for you, Peter, that you would stay faithful to me no matter what comes. Remember this: After you have turned back to me and have been restored, make it your life mission to strengthen the faith of your brothers", (Luke 22:32, The Passion Translation Bible).

This mission that God has given to me is something that I have dreamed of all my life...*to write*. I can remember as a little girl writing poetry, short stories, and even love letters for classmates when I got older; *ANYTHING* I could compose from words to express myself gave me joy! Even when it would be entries in my diary of things that weren't so pleasant, growing up and experiencing life—but it gave me relief, contentment, and pleasure to see my words on paper. I wanted to go to college to learn more about this craft, but was discouraged by others, so I took a different path. But God led me back here—to my purpose—over 50 years later. Oh, what a journey!

In the passage above from the Book of Luke, Jesus is talking to Peter about part of his journey. In The Passion Translation Bible (2020), it explains: "Peter was the first preacher to bring the gospel of Christ to the Jews in Jerusalem. At Pentecost, he stood fearlessly and told the thousands gathered around him that they had denied the Holy One of God and crucified their Messiah. Yet, just 50 days earlier the Apostle Peter, while Jesus was being tried by Pilate, denied that he even knew Jesus… three times. But Jesus *(still)* prophesied beforehand and gave Peter both a Promise and a Commission." The Holy Spirt showed me this one day while I was working on this "Life Work" project, that although part of Peter's journey only covered 50 days and mine 50 years, God's mission for me had not changed—"Make it your life mission to strengthen the faith of your brothers (and sisters)".

Like Peter, I too, denied Christ to live through me as He had purposed before I was conceived. I fought against my true identity for so long that I almost forgot in whom I first believed. I allowed "life" to take control and lord over me—living it beneath the destiny He had created me for. But once I turned back to Him, I knew I could never return to the old life or old way of doing things…*there was more God had in store, and it was time for me to be RESTORED!* As with anything else, restoration is a process, and this project has been a part of mine. I am renewed, I am reformed, I am regenerated, and I am restored! Praise The Living God!

To better understand my journey of being restored, I have to tell the story of how I got here. This is how it happened:

In the summer of 2023, I decided to be a part of a book anthology where I would tell part of my journey of how God brought me through a six-year divorce. My story entry would be the starting point for my first solo *published* book. I knew the project was not just a chance for me to share my testimony of God's goodness, but it was a mandate; a clarion call; MY MISSION. God made it very clear to me on several occasions that He wanted me to finish the book so other women would know God for themselves, and that He can make the impossible, possible. But as I had with other areas of my life, I neglected His mission for me and went about with my own—building my business and network, embarking on other advantageous ventures and more! I would do good for a while, but each year it seemed I would have to start over to get new clients and build them back up. *It was tiresome.* I had paid for coaching programs that were amazing, but as it seemed with everything else, I would start and not complete it. So, I would not reach the full potential I knew was possible.

Fast-forward to August 2024, I finally decided to set a finish date for my book and started working more diligently on it than I had ever done before. But then it happened. (This is my account as written in my article, "*No More Fear, Only Faith*" *I Am Magazine, 2024):*

*"During the Labor Day weekend, I decided to put finishing touches on my book just shy of my goal date, and the inevitable happened...**all of my writing I had worked on for the past months...WAS GONE!** I started a frantic search in all my files, internal and external, looked up ways to retrieve lost files, and solicited the help of my IT guy for a week to "do his magic". I kept positive thoughts, and I refused to say anything negative while the process was still hopeful, but he eventually told me the files*

looked corrupted, and he was not able to retrieve them. Although my emotions—as they had tried before during my wait—wanted to envelope me into sorrow and defeat, I found peace in knowing there was a greater plan for something BIGGER AND BETTER that I had to focus on, (without even knowing what it was). Additionally, during my "waiting period", I had started reading a book that addressed this very thing which prepared me to receive the news that I would pretty much have to start over with my book. The author talked about how he overcame fear and allowed faith to replace it. Oh! How on time it was for me to know this greater plan was what I needed and would end up here to hopefully help someone else do the same!" (Hill, N., 2020, Outwitting the Devil).

Although I didn't agree with all of the philosophies or beliefs in the author's book, he had some real principles that bears mentioning. He shares how his life for a year or so had been lived in total fear—for his very life and well-being. He had come to the end of trying all the ideas his intellect had created—businesses, partnerships, programs with prestigious individuals and institutions. They were mostly successful, but none of them made him happy. *That felt like exactly where I was.* All the business ideas, strategies, attempts I had made, never truly came to full maturity and I was very discontented. And as I was reading the words of the book's author (even while I was **driving** across Alabama from Mississippi to Georgia), *it was as if he was talking directly to me!* "Go back home at once and begin transferring the data you have gathered from your own mind to written manuscript" (Hill, N., 2020, Outwitting the Devil). I WAS CAPTIVATED AND IN TOTAL AMAZEMENT! Instead of hearing the audible words in my mind as he did, *I was reading them out loud to myself as I drove.* That is when I knew, God had something else in mind! As badly as I wanted all of my well-researched, thought out, pages of my other book back, that was not what I was supposed to be working on for that time! I needed to share my **FAITH MINDSET Walk**, which can sometimes mean believing for something and even if you don't get it—knowing God always has something better in mind! Just trust the process.

So, I accept the call and commit my life to God's purpose and plan with my "Mindset of Faith."

My Faith Mindset Walk

This project has been a growth process for me—and there are quite a number of things I have discovered—of myself and of others. First, having a history as a "Christian" is totally different than having the Person of Christ indwelled in you. The Holy Spirit is the Greatest Teacher I have ever had! Most of the key concepts in this manual were downloads inspired directly from Him in "real time". The experience was like working on a life-valued thesis. Different concepts were being revealed to me causing me to do research (in the scriptures, other books, articles, sermons, lessons, etc.) to help me fully understand, for myself first; then, being able to share it in a way that others would grasp and comprehend from my experience. *It was amazing!*

Although the journey was one that I will never forget, it did not come without its challenges. Doing His job, the Holy Spirit has tested me, corrected me, and taken me completely out of my comfort zone; as well as commended, instructed and revealed to me. All of which has been the most rewarding time in my life thus far. Because of the truths I now know about myself and God's Divine Nature and way of doing things, life is so much more complete. That is my prayer for you. This **training manual** that God instructed me to create is here to serve the following purposes: Understanding the Mindset of Faith—its meaning; its foundation; and its purpose for you. It is to /show:

1- Help you understand how faith works (what it is, and what it is not).

2- How your faith has everything to do with your mindset, and how you see yourself, and the world around you.

3- Learn how to interpret the scriptures about faith—learning line upon line, percept upon percept.

4- Help you grasp the concepts for yourself and gain your own revelation of how and what God wants you to see and understand for your own life.

Writing this manual became **My Faith Mindset Walk** when I had to totally abandon my way of doing things and blindly allow Holy Spirit to speak and flow. I gave over my thought processes, my intellect, and my human knowledge to Him, so that I would write exactly what He was downloading—nothing more, nothing less. It became my personal journal first; and then was transformed into **your Faith Mindset Training Manual** you are holding now. Be guided by it, guard and safekeep the revelations you receive from it, and begin to walk out your life in FULL FAITH and trust in God. Because when it all boils down, faith is where you must start—and where you must end.

Now as I said, this is a *training manual*. That means that it is not just a book to read, but it provides concepts that are to be used to train your mindset of faith. There will be work sections for you to complete—with scriptures and more. Make sure to work through each one, because it is designed to help you build on each concept and gain the understanding needed to accomplish its purpose. God has something WONDERFUL waiting for you—so make sure you receive it all!

I want to thank you for allowing me to be a part of your **journey of discovery, transformation, regeneration, and FAITH.** Now, let God's Revealing Truths unlock every mystery that has held you captive—confused, frustrated, feeling ordinary, or inferior. It is time to know who you are and to understand who God is to you, so you can live a FULL SATISFYING LIFE— filling every space and every place of your being with Him! Walk now, in Your Mindset of Faith!

Mindset of Faith—Your Training Manual

Key terms, glossary and references

Key terms are included throughout the chapters, along with a complete glossary and references at the end of this manual to aid in clarity and provide a starting point. BUT do not rely on these alone! God has given you a BRILLIANT MIND and He wants you to use it to its fullest capacity. In fact, this ENTIRE MANUAL is a starting point to get you engaged in learning about your faith, and how to study God's Word. His desire is for you to know Him for *yourself!* Do not **solely** rely on your pastor, your leader, prophets, books, videos, and the like, as your **only** source to know Him! Study to show yourself approved, as the Bible tells us in II Timothy 2:15, *"Do your best to present yourself to God as one approved, a worker who does not need to be ashamed and who correctly handles the word of truth,* (New International Version Bible - NIV). The Holy Spirit is waiting to show you and give you ***your own*** revelation knowledge. Don't deprive yourself of it! START NOW!

1
What is Faith?

Key Terms

Being (State of) – To embody and live out God's Word to the extent that it becomes your identity, nature, and way of life.

God-Consciousness – A mindset focused on God's presence, truth, and divine guidance, shaping thoughts and actions in alignment with His Will.

Infancy (Spiritual) Stage – The beginning phase of a believer's faith journey, marked by basic understanding, reliance on foundational teachings, and gradual growth in spiritual maturity.

Maturity (Spiritual) Stage – A deeper level of faith where a believer operates in full understanding of God's truth, demonstrating spiritual wisdom, discernment, and Christlike character.

Salvation – Preservation or deliverance from sin (harm, ruin or loss-death).

Sonship- Son(s) of God -God's Sons & Daughters – The identity and inheritance of believers as children of God, being asexual (without gender).

Soul Salvation – The process of renewing the mind, will, and emotions through faith in Christ, aligning one's thoughts and actions with God's truth for transformation and wholeness.

True Spirituality – Living in alignment with God's will, walking in faith, and embodying the character of Christ (God).

Simply put, **Faith** *is having complete trust or confidence in someone or something.* It takes root in your heart which is the core of your being; your heart is where it all begins with your desires, beliefs, affections, and convictions. The Passion Translation Bible (TPT) in Proverbs 4:23 says, *"So above all, guard the affections of your heart, for they affect all that you are. Pay attention to the welfare of your innermost being, for from there flows the wellspring of life."* The heart is where faith begins, where God speaks, and where transformation starts.

When you apply faith to your life as a **son of God,** it is the foundation of your relationship with Him. It is the confident assurance and trust in His Word, even when it is not yet visible. That's what the foundational scripture in Hebrews chapter 11 says: "Now faith *is the substance of things hoped for, the evidence of things not seen*" (New King James Version-NKJV). This means that faith is both the assurance of what we hope for and the conviction of realities we cannot yet see with our natural eyes. **Faith begins as**

a seed, planted in your heart when you believe in Jesus, and grows as you live out your relationship with Him. We will explore the seed of faith later.

Take a look at this scripture; Romans 1:17 (TPT)— *"This gospel unveils a continual revelation of God's righteousness— a perfect righteousness given to us when we believe. And it moves us from* **receiving life through faith** *to the* **power of living by faith.**"

This passage of scripture unveils a critical aspect of faith, explaining that it is not static but dynamic—it moves you from receiving life through faith to the power of living by faith. **This verse captures the purpose of this manual: to guide you from the initial moment of faith when you received salvation to a life empowered by faith, where every area of your being—spirit, soul, and body—is transformed.** When you first believed, you entered into a new life, beginning your journey as a child of God. Now, it's time to move from that infant stage to spiritual maturity, where faith shapes how you think, act, and live every day.

God needs you to move to the power of living by faith-NOW. It takes the power of the Living, Resurrected Christ empowering you to activate God's Word in you, so you don't succumb to the powers that rule the world you live in. You have to live by faith now, and not what you see or feel. Now, I will use what I just said and put it into the verse for you—when you believe the gospel (the Good News of your **salvation**), you see (the unveiled) Truth of God and His Righteousness; thereafter you move from just your **soul salvation** of faith to living in the power of a living faith-active, moving, evolving.) That's what NOW FAITH is. It moves you from one level of faith to the next; and to the next; and to the next. It never ceases or stops.

If you have been a Follower of Jesus for a while, and/or connected to a local Body of Christ, you should already know and sense the urgency in the times we live in. I am not a Doom's Day announcer at all however, God is no longer waiting on you to catch up to Him. If you are truly a son of God, He is pulling on you to arise to the place He created you to be in. As His most superior creation, you are destined to rise higher in your living, your thinking, and your behavior; and in doing so, you start to live the life He created for you. Romans 13:11 tells you that, *"Besides this you know what [a critical] hour this is, how it is high time now for you to wake up out of your sleep (roused to reality). For salvation (final deliverance) is nearer to us now than when we first believed (adhered to, trusted in, and relied on Christ, the Messiah)* The Amplified Classic Bible, 2024). Another version says, *"…awaken from your sleep (of spiritual complacency)* The Amplified Bible. What is this telling you? It's telling you that it is possible to live as a Believer in Jesus or a Christian and be asleep *(unaware, dead to, live in ignorance)* to your **true spirituality** and **sonship**—living in your first **infant stage** of salvation, and not moving to the **maturity stage**. This stage of maturity is where you transition from merely believing in Christ to fully living out your faith intentionally and with purpose. It is marked by an active awareness of your identity as a son of God, moving beyond spiritual infancy into a deeper relationship with Him. At this stage, you are no longer satisfied with surface-level faith; instead, you embrace a mindset rooted in God's word, wisdom, and power.

Maturity in faith means walking in the fullness of **God-Consciousness,** *where your thoughts align with His thoughts, and your actions reflect His will.* It is the stage where your faith becomes *Now Faith*—a dynamic, present-tense reliance on God that transforms every aspect of your life. You grow from believing to *being!* This refers to embodying and living out God's Word to the extent that it becomes your identity, nature, and way of life. It means allowing God's Word to transform your thoughts, actions, and character until you become a living expression of His truth, love, and righteousness. Just as Jesus was the Word made flesh (John 1:14), sons of God are called to manifest the Word through their lives—not just know it but *be it.*

This mature faith is not about perfection but progression, as you continuously grow in understanding, obedience, and trust in God's plan.

Your Work

What does faith mean to you and how can you apply it daily to mature in it?

_____
_____
_____
_____
_____
_____
_____
_____
_____
_____
_____
_____
_____
_____
_____
_____
_____

Faith is More than Belief

How Belief Clings

Faith and belief, while closely related, are not the same. *Belief is something you hold tightly to—a conviction or idea you build your thoughts and life around.* As Alan Watts (2011) once said, "Belief clings. Faith lets go." Belief often feels safe—it's structured, concrete, and something you can grasp for security. *You cling (hold on) to it for dear life!*

When I picture something *clinging*, I see a dryer sheet sticking to a pair of pants. Dryer sheets are used to *reduce* static cling (*neutralize negative charges*) and *balance out* electrons and ions that cause static. So, when we *believe* in something, *it only reduces the negative charges* which helps to balance us out. *This is a good place to start.* So, BELIEVING is just the first step in developing faith.

Google (2024) states that, belief means- *an acceptance that a statement is true or that something exists; Something someone accepts as true or real; a firm held opinion or conviction, i.e. To the best of my belief (knowledge); in the belief that.* When you believe in something, you accept it to be true and that it exists. You may say, "Yes, I believe in God, and I accept His existence to be real or true." So that you clearly and definitively understand the difference for yourself, complete the sentence below. (Examples of things or people you believe in. An example, "I believe that if I drop this book, it will fall to the floor." Or "I believe that Jesus died and rose again on the 3rd day".) Your turn.

"I believe that..." **Finish this sentence:**

_____
_____
_____
_____
_____
_____
_____
_____
_____
_____
_____
_____
_____
_____

This represents some of the things/people you believe in. Now, using my example above with the definition of belief, this is what I see:

"I believe that if I drop this book, it will fall to the floor because I accept the statement about the Law of Gravity and that it is true, it is a fact, and it

exists". (I have seen it in action, and it does work). I cling to my belief. Once you discover a principle you strongly trust and believe in, it then becomes a core belief, and you begin to build an entire **system** of thinking around it.

A System of Belief

When these beliefs shape how you interact with others, how you see yourself and the world at large, it becomes something that you use as a life guide. *A **core belief** is a deeply held, foundational conviction that is often developed early in life and serves as the underlying principles that influence thoughts, emotions, behaviors, and decision-making.* Core beliefs can be positive or negative and are usually so ingrained that they operate unconsciously, guiding a person's reactions to life experiences. These core beliefs can influence relationships, career choices, and overall life satisfaction. They often serve as the foundation for other values and attitudes, and they can evolve over time through self-reflection, life experiences, or personal growth.

As these core beliefs connect and intertwine into your thoughts and behaviors, they then form what is called a belief system. A **belief system** is *a set of codes, principles, values, and ideologies that individuals hold, often shaped by cultural, societal, religious, and personal influences* (Oxfordreview.com, 2025). Your belief system can be considered as "The invisible force behind your behavior" (Tim Rettig, 2017). This system forms the lens through which you perceive the world and influences how you function and form your understanding of *EVERYTHING!* It is usually based on teachings, doctrines, or philosophical perspectives.

The Rewire Process

Key Term

New Faith System – Letting go of fear-based thinking and embracing a faith-centered perspective that empowers you to walk in purpose.

Because of this interconnectedness of your beliefs (belief system), any change will activate a chain reaction in the system. As stated by Tim Rettig (2017) in an online blog, **"A change in one belief will affect the (entire) system. If it is a core belief, a change can potentially lead to the disruption of the system as a whole. If there is a change in a set of beliefs, other parts of the system will have to rearrange in order to rebuild the coherence (consistency) of the system."** This is a phenomenon when it comes to your mindset, and how you allow faith to take over where belief stops! This is my interpretation:

If you have a set of beliefs that do not align with God's Word, (what He says of you and who He created you to be), but you allow ONE CHANGE in your thoughts and mindset, a chain reaction occurs and your entire belief system starts rearranging and rebuilding to create your **NEW FAITH SYSTEM**, thus a change in mindset! YES! This means you can move from believing God can do something for you, to "**I CAN DO ALL THINGS** through Christ that strengthens me!" (Philippians 4:13,

NKJV). So, if you commit to a complete set of beliefs to change, your current belief system will be rearranged in order to rebuild consistency of your New Faith System. In other words, **everything changes! That is GOOD NEWS!**

Creating A New Faith System

A Moment of Transparency

I have always found comfort in familiarity. Like many people, I had routines, thought patterns, and beliefs that shaped how I saw the world. These patterns felt safe, predictable, and, at times, even unshakable. However, as I started on my faith journey, I realized that many of these beliefs were actually limiting me rather than empowering me.

One of the biggest challenges I faced was letting go of old mindsets—especially those shaped by fear, past disappointments, and self-doubt. Rewiring my mind meant unlearning what I thought was true and allowing God's truth to reshape my thinking.

At first, I resisted. Change felt uncomfortable, even threatening. I had built an entire identity around what I thought was possible for me. But as I leaned into faith, I discovered that my resistance was only making the process harder. The more I fought, the more I struggled. The more I let go, the easier it became to embrace transformation.

I began to understand that my old belief system was based on past experiences and emotions, but God was calling me to build a *new faith system*—one that operated from a place of trust in His Word rather than my own understanding.

The Process of Rewiring

Rewiring your mind is not an overnight process. It requires:

- Recognizing limiting beliefs that keep you bound.
- Replacing old thoughts with faith-filled declarations.
- Realigning your mindset with God's Word.
- Reinforcing your faith system daily through scripture, prayer, and intentional actions.

Romans 12:2 tells you: *"And do not be conformed to this world, but be transformed by the renewing of your mind…" (NKJV).*

This renewal is the foundation of your New Faith System. It's about letting go of fear-based thinking and embracing a faith-centered perspective that empowers you to walk in purpose.

Your New Faith System Starts Today

If you find yourself stuck in old thought patterns, know this: **You have the power to rewire your mind.** You don't have to stay trapped in fear, doubt, or past failures. You can create a new faith system that aligns with God's truth, empowering your decisions, and strengthening your walk with Him.

Your Work

What are some things in your life that you fight to change? List them below:

_____
_____
_____
_____
_____
_____
_____
_____
_____
_____
_____
_____
_____
_____
_____
_____
_____
_____
_____
_____
_____
_____

What are some ways you can rewire your mind from having a belief system to becoming a FAITH SYSTEM? List scriptures to help you do this.

_____

_____

_____

_____

_____

_____

_____

_____

_____

_____

_____

_____

_____

_____

_____

_____

_____

_____

_____

_____

How Faith LET'S GO

With faith, you can *LET GO*. You let go and have freedom with God by TOTALLY trusting Him. You have no preconceived *notions of facts*, blocking your vision of knowing *truths*. Faith goes beyond belief. Faith requires you to trust, surrender, and take action. It calls you to let go of your need for control and rely entirely on God, even when you can't see the outcome. In fact, *Faith is what pleases God, not belief.* Hebrews 11:6 says, *"And without faith it is impossible to please God…"* (New International Version, NIV Bible). Your beliefs can change because they depend on human experience and knowledge. FAITH on the other hand, is born from God. It is the innate divine wisdom that was already inside of you before you were born. It is as a seed—as The Bible says in Matthew 17:20a, *("…if you have faith inside of you no bigger than the size of a small mustard seed…"* (TPT Bible), therefore it must *grow*. It carries life and produces life. As a noun— faith is a gift. Ephesians 2:8 states that, "For by grace you have been saved through faith, and this is not from you; It is the gift of God," (NIV). As a verb— faith is active. James 2:17 in The Passion Translation Bible says, *"So then faith that doesn't involve action is phony"*. It requires you to do something about it to prove it is real!

Now Faith Is

The Book of Hebrews, chapter 11 has always been the Foundation of Faith, its meaning and showing examples of the prophets of old that lived by faith. The very first verse says, "*NOW faith is…*". It is in *the now*. Faith is the act of moving forward with confidence, even when you cannot see where the path will lead. It is revealed as you are walking it out. You must *endure (to remain in existence; to last)* in it—continuing your course of action even in the face of difficulty. Reading Hebrews in *The Passion Translation Bible* gave me a whole new meaning of the word—FAITH. Before I could even turn to the chapter, I was drawn to the introduction of the book and found out some history and background on the Book of Hebrews. This is one of the beautifully articulated quotes below:

"Nowhere is there a better definition and explanation of faith in the New Testament then in the sermon letter of Hebrews. **Now Faith brings our hopes into reality and becomes <u>the foundation</u> needed to acquire the things we long for. It is <u>all the evidence required</u> to prove what is still unseen,** *(Hebrews 11:1). This is a far cry from the traditional understanding that faith is merely belief. Biblical Faith claims a confidence beyond our own because it rests in* **The Character of God, (which is) THE FOUNDATION of our Faith**. *Part of practicing faith is persevering in it (The Passion Translation -TPT).*

In Hebrews 11:6, the book goes on to say, *"And without faith living within us it would be impossible to please God. For we come to God in faith knowing that He is real and that He rewards the faith of those who passionately seek Him" (TBT).* This solidifies the exquisite definition in verse one. Faith is what God requires of us; and as we seek Him, we are rewarded for our diligence. To get the full meaning here, let's break this down a little bit more.

1- Faith brings our hopes INTO reality. Hope means- A feeling of expectation and desire for a certain thing to happen; a feeling of trust. It is **an optimistic state of mind** that is based on **an expectation of positive outcomes** with respect to events and circumstances in one's life or the world at large (Dictionary.com and Wikipedia definition).

For short, **HOPE IS AN EXPECTATION AND DESIRE FROM AN OPTIMISTIC STATE OF MIND FOR POSITIVE OUTCOMES.** Now let's substitute this in the verse above:

"**Faith brings an expectation and desire from an optimistic state of mind for positive outcomes INTO reality!**" This is part of the process of *renewing your mind* and having a *regenerated mindset (a shift in thought patterns/beliefs through the Holy Spirit, resulting in a faith-driven, God-centered life),* that replaces your old mindset that we will talk about later.

2- (Faith) becomes THE FOUNDATION needed to acquire the things we long for. Remember earlier when I shared that everything started with receiving life through faith? Becoming a follower of Christ Jesus, starts with having faith, so naturally it is the foundation of your Faith (Mindset) Walk. This explains that *faith is what you need to get the things in life you long for (desire/yearn).*

So, the question to answer now is:

What do you long for?

A Moment of Transparency

Here is my transparent moment on this topic: *I am preparing for my husband to find me.* It took a very long time for me to admit this to myself, and even longer for me to SAY OUT LOUD. This process is part of my preparation for him: Learning to talk to him in the spirit realm out loud. I am purposefully telling you this because *whatever the things are that you long for* you have to tell them you long for them—and YES, you have to say it out loud to start creating your atmosphere to prepare to receive them.

Believe me, before I came to this realization, I was not acting like I was ready. I was "living my life" on my terms, and that was leading me nowhere fast! It wasn't until I relinquished my whole being over to God and started to make different choices, then I understood that *speaking my truth was about speaking my faith!* And from there I started to mature in the ways and thoughts of God, through His Word- which allowed my relationship with Christ to go deeper. Colossians 1:23 (TPT) states, *"If indeed you continue to advance in faith, assured of a firm foundation to grow upon. Never be shaken from the hope of the gospel you have believed in."* This verse encourages you to remain steadfast, refusing to let the challenges of life shake you from your firm foundation of faith. Instead, it calls you to keep advancing, growing, and maturing in your faith. That means your faith should always be improving, moving to higher levels, causing bigger miracles, expanding how you think and respond to circumstances and situations. It is constantly activating God's Word to be performed in your life! This is the essence of what the Lord declares in Jeremiah 1:12 (The Amplified Bible): "Then said the Lord to me, you have seen well, for I am alert and active, watching over My Word to perform it." When we place our faith in God's Word by believing it, speaking it, and acting on it, He is faithful to ensure that it comes to pass.

The Word of God: The Incorruptible Seed of Faith

When you speak of faith, you must first recognize that *faith originates from the Word of God.* Just as a seed carries within it the potential for life, *God's Word is the incorruptible seed* that produces faith (life) within you.

The Bible speaks of the ***incorruptible seed*** *(God's Word that becomes the seed of faith planted in you when you receive salvation)* in **1 Peter 1:22-23 (TPT)**:

"Now because of your obedience to the truth, you have purified your very souls, and this empowers you to be full of love for your fellow believers. So, express this sincere love toward one another passionately and with a pure heart. For through The Eternal and Living Word of God you have been born again. And this 'seed' that He planted within you can never be destroyed and will live and grow inside of you forever."

This passage is powerful for understanding faith! Let's break it down and connect it to how faith develops in your life.

1- The Word of God is the first seed planted in you

The Eternal and Living Word of God is the first seed that takes root in your heart. When you first hear and receive the message of salvation, this divine seed is planted. It is incorruptible, meaning it cannot decay, fade, or lose its power. The moment you accept Christ, this seed is deposited into your spirit (heart), but like any seed, it requires nourishment to grow.

Romans 10:17 (NKJV) says,

"Faith comes by hearing, and hearing by the Word of God."

Notice that it does not say, "…hearing the Word of God", but "…hearing **BY** *the Word of God*". This means that it takes more than just hearing with your natural ears, you must hear BY God's Word, planted inside you. It must *take root*. Faith is not an abstract concept—it is a living force that grows as you continue to hear, meditate on, and apply The Word of God. Just as a tree starts as a seed, your faith journey begins with the implanted Word of God.

2- The seed of faith produces the Fruit of the Spirit

Once The Word of God takes root inside of you, it begins to grow your faith. Faith is not meant to be stagnant—it is designed to grow, transforming you from the inside out. Faith then shows the evidence of its dynamic power producing fruit that is seen by all.

Galatians 5:22-23 (TPT) describes this transformation:

"But the fruit produced by the Holy Spirit within you is divine love in all its varied expressions. Joy that overflows, peace that subdues, patience that endures, kindness in action, a life full of virtue, faith that prevails, gentleness of heart, and strength of spirit. Never set the law above these qualities, for they are meant to be limitless."

As the seed of faith grows in your heart, it produces fruit ***(Fruit of the Spirit)**—the evidence of God's Spirit at work in you.* This includes *love, joy, peace, patience, kindness, goodness, faithfulness, gentleness, and self-control.* These are not just qualities we strive for—they are the spiritual evident proof of a faith-filled life.

Imagine a tree:

- **The Word is the seed.**
- **Faith** is the sprout.
- **The Fruit of the Spirit** is the evidence of growth, showing the world that God's life is inside you.

3- Living the Life God Desires for You

When the incorruptible seed of The Word of God has been planted and faith has taken root, you begin to live the full, abundant life that God desires for you.

John 10:10b (NKJV) says: *"I have come that they may have life, and that they may have it more abundantly."*

God's plan is not for you to live in lack, fear, or defeat, but to thrive—spiritually, emotionally, financially, and physically. Through faith, you access every spiritual and physical blessing that is rightfully yours as a son of God.

- **Faith unlocks your inheritance in Christ.**
- **Faith empowers you to walk in victory.**
- **Faith leads you into a life of purpose, prosperity, and divine success.**

The Word of God is the incorruptible seed that, when received, produces faith—a faith that grows and manifests as the Fruit of the Spirit, leading you to a life of abundance and purpose.

Your Work:

Are you nurturing the seed God has planted within you? If yes, how are you achieving this? If not, what can you do today to start?

_____
_____
_____
_____
_____
_____
_____
_____
_____
_____
_____
_____
_____
_____
_____
_____
_____
_____

What are you doing to allow faith to grow and transform your life?

NOTES

2

The Power in Bold Faith

Key Terms

Character of God – The unchanging nature and attributes of God, including His love, faithfulness, righteousness, mercy, and justice.

God's Kingdom – (God as **King**, has **dominion** over all). The sovereign reign and rule of God as King over all creation—both in heaven and on earth.

Mindset of Faith – A mental and spiritual posture that fully trusts in God's Word, character, and assurances, regardless of circumstances.

Sovereignty – The supreme power and authority of God to rule over all creation.

Spirit-Revealed Truths – Divine insights and understanding of God's Word imparted by the Holy Spirit that go beyond intellectual knowledge.

As I revisited Hebrews Chapter 11 in *The Passion Translation* Bible, I gained a fresh revelation about the nature and power of faith. This chapter, often referred to as the "Hall of Faith," provides a vivid portrayal of faith in action through the lives of biblical heroes. Their stories go beyond mere belief, demonstrating faith as a vibrant force that drives obedience, courage, and perseverance. The following analysis explores these examples, breaking down how faith manifests in practical ways and how it shapes a life of purpose and trust in God. Through this study, you will see how faith, when actively lived out, becomes the groundwork for fulfilling God's Plan and advancing His **kingdom**. The following is the breakdown analysis for your study.

Hebrews Chapter 11 – The Analysis

Reference: The Passion Translation Bible, 2020

Verse 1 (V1)- Now faith brings our hopes into reality and becomes the foundation needed to acquire the things we long for. It is all the evidence required to prove what is still unseen.

V2- This testimony of faith is what previous generations were commended for.

V3- **Faith empowers** us to see that the universe was created and beautifully coordinated by the power of God's Words! He spoke and the invisible realm gave birth to all that is seen.

Empowers- Gives authority in power to do something; to make more confident and stronger. *Faith gives authority and power to you to do something, making you more confident and stronger.*

V4- Faith moved Abel to choose a more acceptable sacrifice to offer God than his brother Cain, and God declared him righteous because of his offering of faith. By his faith, Abel still speaks instruction to us today, even though he is long dead.

Moves- Go in a specified direction or manner; change position (mindset); making progress and develop in a particular manner or direction. *Faith moves in a specific direction (ascends) to change your position (mindset); develops your new mindset.*

V5- Faith translated Enoch from this life and he was taken up into heaven! He never had to experience death; he just disappeared from this world because God promoted him. For before he was translated to the heavenly realm his life had become a pleasure to God.

Translates- Express the sense of words in another language; moves from one place or condition to another. *Faith expresses in another language (your new language) of words that moves (you) from one place (your old mindset) or condition to another (your new mindset).*

V6- And without faith living in us it would be impossible to please God. For we come to God in faith knowing that He is real and that He rewards the faith of those who passionately seek Him.

V7- **Faith opened** Noah's heart to receive revelation and warnings from God about what was coming, even things that had never been seen. But he stepped out in reverent obedience to God and built an ark that would save him and his family. By his faith the world was condemned, but Noah received God's gift of righteousness that comes by believing.

Opens- Allowing access, passage, or view through an (empty) space; not closed or blocked up. *Faith allows access passage(way) to something that can be viewed; it (your mindset) is no longer closed or blocked but it's free to flow and let go.*

V8- **Faith motivated** Abraham to obey God's call and leave the familiar to discover the territory he was destined to inherit from God. So, he left with only a promise and without even knowing ahead of time where he was going, Abraham stepped out in faith.

Motivates- Provides a motive for doing something. **Motive**- the reason for it—hidden or unseen; not obvious to the natural eye or senses. *Faith provides a reason or cause to do something; especially when the reason is hidden or not obvious or not* seen. *(To ignore the obvious -the issue- and focus on what is hidden and unseen-Faith as the solution).*

V9- He (Abraham) **lived by faith** as an immigrant in his promised land as though it belonged to someone else. He journeyed through the land living in tents with Isaac and Jacob who were persuaded that they were also co-heirs of the same promise.

To Live (Life; A Way of Life)- A condition for the capacity to grow; to produce; to have functional activity and continuous change. *Faith is a condition for the capacity to grow, to reproduce, to have functional activity, and continuous change.*

V10- His (Abraham's) **eyes of faith** were set on the city with unshakable foundations, whose architect and builder is God Himself.

See (faith sees)- Discern or deduce mentally after reflection or from information; to understand. *Faith discerns mentally (after serious thought and consideration), through reflection to gain understanding.*

V11a- Sarah's **faith embraced** God's miracle power to conceive even though she was barren and was past the age of childbearing...

Embrace- To accept or support (a belief, theory, or change) willingly and enthusiastically. *Faith accepts or supports a belief, theory, or change willingly and enthusiastically.*

V11b- ...for the **authority of her** (Sarah's) **faith** rested in The One who made the promise and she tapped into His faithfulness.

Authority- The power or the right to give orders, make decisions, and enforce obedience. *Faith has the power or the right to give orders, make decisions, and enforce obedience.* (That means once you operate in faith, whatever the situation is, it has no other choice than to be obedient to YOUR faith).

V12-16- In fact, so many children were subsequently fathered by this aged man of faith- one who was as good as dead, that he now has offspring as innumerable as the sand on the seashore and as the stars in the sky! These heroes all died still clinging to their faith, not even receiving all that had been promised to them. But they saw beyond the horizon the fulfillment of their promises and gladly embraced it from afar. *They all lived their lives on earth as those who belonged to another realm.* For clearly, those who live this way are longing for the appearing of a heavenly city. And if their hearts were still remembering what they left behind, they would have found an opportunity to go back. **But they couldn't turn back** for their hearts were **fixed** on what was far greater, that is, the heavenly realm! So because of this God is not ashamed in any way to be called their God, for He has prepared a heavenly city for them.

Fixed- Fastened securely in place; (of a person's expression) held for a long time without changing, especially to conceal other feelings. *Faith is fastened securely in place (in your heart); it is a long-held expression that does not change, (despite) how you feel.*

V17-19- **Faith operated** powerfully in Abraham for when he was put to the test he offered up Isaac. Even though he received God's promises of descendants, he was willing to offer up his only son! For God had promised (to Abraham), "through your son Isaac your lineage will carry on your name." Abraham's faith made it logical to him that God could raise Isaac from the dead and symbolically that's exactly what happened.

Operate/Operation- A system or machine that has to be worked and put to the test. *Faith is a system that has to be worked and put to the test.*

V20- The **Power of Faith** prompted Isaac to impart a blessing to his sons, Jacob and Esau, concerning their prophetic destinies.

Power- The ability to do something or act in a particular way; the capacity or ability to direct or influence the behavior of others or course of events. *Faith has the ability to do something or act in a particular way; faith has the capacity and the ability to* *direct and influence the behavior of others or course of events.*

V21- Jacob worshipped in **faith's reality** at the end of his life, and leaning upon his staff he imparted a prophetic blessing upon each of Joseph's sons.

Reality (State of Mind)- The world or state of things as they actually exist; the state or quality of having existence or substance. *Faith's quality of substance is how things actually exist.*

V22- **Faith inspired** Joseph and opened his eyes to see into the future, for as he was dying he prophesied about the exodus of Israel out of Egypt and gave instructions that his bones were to be taken from Egypt with them.

Inspires- Fill with the urge or ability to do something; breathe into. *Faith fills (you) with the urge and the ability to do something, and breaths into (you) to bring life.*

V23- **Faith prompted** the parents of Moses at his birth to hide him for three months, because they realized their child was exceptional and they refused to be afraid of the King's edict.

Prompt- An event or fact that causes or brings about an action; assists or encourages to say or do something. *Faith changes or* *brings about an action to assist and encourages to say or do something.*

V24-25a- **Faith enabled** Moses to choose God's will, for although he was raised as the son of Pharaoh's daughter, he refused to make that his identity, choosing instead to suffer mistreatment with the people of God.

Enable- Gives authority or means to do something; make operational or activate. *Faith gives the authority and the means to do something; It is operational, and it activates.*

V25b- Moses preferred **faith's certainty** above the momentary enjoyment of sin's pleasures.

Certainty- A firm conviction that something is the case; The quality of being reliably true; A fact that is definitely true or an event that is definitely going to take place. *Faith is a firm conviction that something is definitely true or definitely going to take place.*

V26- He (Moses) found his true wealth, in suffering abuse for being anointed, more than in anything the world could offer him, for his eyes looked with wonder not on the immediate, but on the ultimate—**faith's great reward!**

Reward- A thing given in recognition of one's service, effort, or achievement. *Faith gives recognition of one's service, effort, or achievement.*

V27- Holding **faith's promise** Moses abandoned Egypt and had no fear of Pharaoh's rage because he persisted in faith as if he had seen God who is unseen.

Promise- A declaration or assurance that one will do a particular thing or that a particular thing will happen. *Faith is a declaration or assurance that one (you) will do a particular thing, or a particular thing will happen.*

V28- **Faith stirred** Moses to perform the rite of Passover and sprinkle lamb's blood, to protect the destroyer from harming their firstborn.

Stir- To move around and mix thoroughly; Move or causes to move. *Faith causes movement (increasing) your trust in God.*

V29- **Faith opened** the way for the Hebrews to cross the Red Sea as if on dry land, but when the Egyptians tried to cross they were swallowed up and drowned!

Open- (See Verse 7- open)

V30- **Faith pulled** down Jericho's walls after the people marched around them for seven days!

Pull- Exert force on someone or something so as to cause movement towards oneself; to move in a specified direction with effort especially by taking hold of something. *Faith exerts force to cause movement towards oneself (you) especially by taking hold of something.*

V31- **Faith provided** a way of escape for Rahab the prostitute, avoiding the destruction of the unbelievers, because she received the Hebrews spies in peace.

Provide- Makes available for use or supplies; make adequate preparation for. *Faith makes available and supplies adequate preparation for whatever you need.*

V32-33a- And what more could I say to convince you? For there is not enough time to tell you of the faith of Gideon, Barak, Samson, Jephthah, David, Samuel, and the prophets. Through faith's power they conquered kingdoms and established true justice.

V33b- Their **faith fastened** onto their promises and pulled them (their promises) into reality! It was faith that shut the mouth of lions..."

Fastens- Close or do up securely; Single out and concentrate on; direct one's eyes, thoughts, etc. intently at. *Faith closes (doubt out) securely; it concentrates and directs one's eyes and thoughts intently at something (Christ Jesus).*

V34a- "...put out the power of raging fire, and caused many to escape certain death by the sword. Although weak, their faith imparted power to make them strong!

V34b- **Faith sparked** courage within them and they became mighty warriors in battle, pulling armies from another realm into battle array.

Spark- Produced by striking together; Trace of a specified quality or intense feeling; to ignite. *Faith ignites a specified quality and intensity.*

V35a- **Faith-filled** women saw their dead children raised in resurrection power. Yet it was faith that enabled others to endure great atrocities.

Fills- Causes to become full; become an overwhelming presence in. *Faith causes you to be full and takes you into the overwhelming presence of God.*

V35b-39-They were stretched out on the wheel and tortured and didn't deny their faith in order to be freed, because they *longed for* a more honorable and glorious resurrection! Others were mocked and experienced the most severe beating with whips; they were in chains and imprisoned. Some of these faith champions were brutally killed by stoning, being sawn in two or slaughtered by the sword. These lived in faith as they went about wearing goatskins and sheepskins for clothing. They lost everything they possessed, they endured great afflictions, and they were cruelly mistreated. They wandered the earth living in the desert wilderness, in caves, on barren mountains and in holes in the earth. Truly, the world was not even worthy of them, not realizing who they were. These were the true heroes, commended for their faith, yet they lived in hope without receiving the fullness of what was promised them.

V40- But now God has invited us to live in something better than what they had— **faith's fullness.**

Fullness- State of being filled to capacity. *Faith fills you to capacity leaving no room for anything else (fear).*

Analysis Overview of Faith

DID YOU HEAR THAT?! FAITH does and is a LOT of things! This breakdown provides the explanation of what faith is and how to work it! Let's take a closer look now. I want to give an example of how to use the verbs you just read, apply them and put them to work.

Example: You have always wanted to start a business of your own, doing what you love. However, you are the sole breadwinner for your family and must have constant revenue coming in for the livelihood of you and your family. *How do you apply faith to be able to do this?*

I will share some of the principles from above to explain this example.

The reference scripture says in Hebrews 11:1, which starts the chapter off stating, *The end result in the beginning*. The statement is that, *"Now Faith brings our hopes into reality and becomes the foundation needed to acquire the things we long for. It is all the evidence required to prove what is still unseen"* (TPT).

It is actually telling you what faith is, before you read and **SEE** the examples of it from the Champions of Faith. You must see it **now** before you even read about what faith did for them. Because—**FAITH IS NOW!** Therefore, to start that business you so desire, you must **see it first**; that includes doing things to prepare for it (saving money, improving your credit, making contacts, and putting things in place, etc.)

Remember the breakdown of this earlier? *Faith brings an expectation and desire from an optimistic state of mind for positive outcomes INTO reality!* So, this is where you must begin BEFORE you leave your job to start your business. Change your mindset from a mindset of fear (doubt and uncertainty) to an optimistic mindset of *what faith does:*

IT EMPOWERS YOU and *gives you the authority and* ***power*** *to do it, making you more confident and stronger.* ***Power*** *has the capacity and the ability to direct and influence your behavior and course of events.*

IT OPENS (Your Mind) to allow free flowing access to something when you LET GO of your old mindset.

IT MOTIVATES YOU providing a reason to do that which is hidden and not obviously seen.

IT TESTS YOU after you put it's operation to work.

IT INSPIRES YOU and fills you with the urge and the ability to do it.

IT PROMPTS YOU and brings about action to encourage you to do it.

IT GIVES YOU CERTAINTY with a firm conviction that something is definitely going to take place.

IT PROMISES YOU with a declaration that it will happen.

IT PULLS YOU by exerting force to cause your desire to move towards you, especially when you take hold of the thought of the **reality** that it actually exists.

IT FASTENS TO YOU and closes doubt out securely as you concentrate and direct your eyes and thoughts intently at it.

And more!!!

YOUR FAITH IS JUST THAT POWERFUL—AND SO ARE YOU! This is how to activate your faith and put it to work! But you must remember that it is THE WORD OF GOD that causes the "Seed of Faith" to grow in you to produce the activity of these. Now you will learn how the Seed of Faith works. Before you do, complete your work below.

Your Work

What are some ways you can implement faith into your life for what you desire?

_____
_____
_____
_____
_____
_____
_____
_____
_____
_____
_____
_____

What is your new knowledge about faith after reading the section above? Write your answer below.

_____
_____
_____
_____
_____
_____
_____

NOTES

3

Faith IS a Mindset

Key Terms

Character of God – The unchanging nature and attributes of God, including His love, faithfulness, righteousness, mercy, and justice.

God's Kingdom – (God as **King**, has **dominion** over all). The sovereign reign and rule of God as King over all creation—both in heaven and on earth.

Mindset of Faith – A mental and spiritual posture that fully trusts in God's Word, character, and assurances, regardless of circumstances.

Sovereignty – The supreme power and authority of God to rule over all creation.

Spirit-Revealed Truths – Divine insights and understanding imparted by the Holy Spirit that go beyond intellectual knowledge.

Understanding what faith is and how it works is very important in developing your mindset for it. Once faith is established in your heart, it then starts to shape how you think, perceive, and respond to life. It is not just about believing what God said but aligning your thoughts with His Word and trusting His Character as your firm foundation. Because *His Word depicts His Character*—your mindset must be rooted in His Word by faith, so that you are empowered to see beyond the natural and operate with confidence in the unseen realities of **God's Kingdom**. This foundational mindset transforms your perspective, enabling you to grow and mature in your faith as you advance toward God's purpose for your life. Developing this mindset is the first step to living a life where faith is not just a belief but a way of thinking, acting, and being. This ***mindset of faith*** is the power that you live your life by; it preserves you, as you allow God's Word to penetrate your entire being—Your Spirit, Your Body, and YOUR MIND.

Proverbs 4:21-22 says, *"Fill your thoughts with my words until they penetrate deep into your spirit. Then as you unwrap my words they will impart true life and radiant health into the very core of your being"* (TPT). Faith in God's Word only starts to work for you *after* you allow it to *penetrate* your entire being! The word *"penetrate"* means to succeed in forcing a way into or through (a thing); success in understanding or gaining insight into (something complex or mysterious). So, in essence, God's Word must be *forced* into you to gain insight into God's complexity—His Thoughts and Ways.

A Moment of Transparency

The word *forced* sounds like a strong word to use, but in some cases, that is exactly what happens. For me, I have not always chosen the "easy road". I made choices that ended up making my life more difficult than it needed to be. But once I made up my mind that I needed God back in my life, there was no turning back! However, it is a daily choice to "Walk the Walk". After years of letting my heart grow hard, God's Word, in its loving precision, had to break through forcefully to reach and transform my heart. My eyes are now open to His **Spirit Revealed Truths** causing The Mystery of God's Mind to now be my mind! And now, it's time for this Mind of God to also be in you! (Philippians 2:5, *"Let this mind be in you which was also in Christ Jesus,"* NKJV Bible).

Your Work

What can you do different (starting today) to allow God's Word to penetrate your heart?

_____
_____
_____
_____
_____
_____
_____
_____
_____
_____
_____
_____
_____
_____
_____
_____
_____
_____
_____
_____

Your Faith Mindset *is* God's Character

Faith is not just about believing; it's about knowing who God is, trusting His character, and relying on His unchanging nature as the foundation for your confidence. Your faith mindset is grounded in the **Character of God**, how He sees you, how you see yourself, and how you see the world around you. Biblical faith goes beyond intellectual agreement. It calls us to trust in God's character—His goodness, faithfulness, and **sovereignty**. When you know who God is, your faith becomes unwavering, even in the face of uncertainty. It is not rooted in circumstances or personal strength but in the steadfast character of God Himself. His character—faithful, loving, just, and true—provides the stability and assurance you need to keep moving forward. This firm foundation empowers you to mature in your faith, transforming it into a vibrant, living force that impacts every area of your life and the lives of those you are connected to. Faith, rooted in the mindset of God's character, becomes the anchor that holds you steady and the momentum that pushes you toward God's purpose for your life.

Now, let's go a little deeper into God's Character and Who He is.

The Character of God is in His Name (Who He is)

- **SEES ALL (El Roi)**
- **IS EVERYWHERE (Jehovah-Shammah)**

- **IS THE BEGINNING and THE END (Alpha and Omega)**
- **IS CREATOR OF EVERYTHING (ELOHIM)**
- **IS THE LIVING GOD (EL CHAY)**

The simplest way I can explain Who God Is, is by listing what His Name means. He is such an ALL-ENCOMPASSING GOD, that I would be here writing until the pages ceased to be added and letters ran out! Since you know that is realistically impossible, then you know that God's existence *IS NEVER-ENDING*. God's character is revealed through His many names, each one reflecting a different aspect of His Nature and how He interacts with His people. These names are not mere titles; they are windows into the depths of who He is, providing you with a glimpse of His attributes, His power, His love, and His faithfulness. When you understand the meaning behind God's names, you begin to see the multifaceted nature of His character. This understanding is essential for your faith because it strengthens your trust in Him, knowing that His Word is grounded in His eternal, unchanging nature.

For the purpose of this discussion on faith, I will only highlight a few of His names that directly tie into gaining more understanding of trust, belief, and reliance in His Word.

Five Meanings and Names of God

1- El Roi, The God Who Sees- Genesis 16:13

This comes from the story of Abraham and Sarah and her handmaiden Hagar. Sarah convinced Abraham to conceive a child with Hagar to "help God out" because they thought Sarah was too old to bear the promised child to them. Sarah became disgruntled with Hagar (before/after having Ismael—the son she bore for Abraham), causing Hagar to run into the wilderness. But God sent an angel to her there, to give her comfort and to speak of God's grace and mercy. Hagar, then says in this passage of scripture, *"Thereafter, Hagar used another name to refer to the LORD, who had spoken to her. She said, "You are the God who sees me." She also said, "Have I truly seen the One who sees me?"* (New Living Translation Bible, NLT).

God wants you to know, *He sees you* and your faith towards Him. You make it the foundation of your life and He is pleased!

Your Work

Find a reference scripture that fits you and what you desire. What scripture(s) lets you know God sees you? Write it/them out below.

_____
_____
_____
_____
_____
_____

2- Jehovah-Shammah, The Lord is There- Psalm 139:7

This verse asks, "Where could I go from Your Spirit? Where could I run and hide from Your Face?" (TBT). Because God is Omnipresent (He is everywhere all the time at the same time), there is NOWHERE you can go and He does not know it. No matter what amount of faith you have or not, God meets you where you are and brings you into Himself.

What scripture(s) tells you God is there with you? Write it/them out below.

3- Alpha and Omega, The Beginning and the End- Revelation 22:13

In this book of Revelation, Jesus said, *"I am the Alpha and the Omega, the First and the Last, the Beginning and the End,"* (NLT Bible). Alpha is the first letter of the Greek alphabet, and Omega is the last. In our language today, Jesus is saying, "I am A through Z." That means, He is at your beginning, your end—AND BETWEEN! Your trust in Him shows you have faith that no matter what comes your way, you know God's got your back, your front, and on every side!

What scripture(s) reminds you that God is your beginning and your end? Write it/them out below.

_____
_____
_____
_____
_____
_____
_____
_____
_____
_____
_____
_____

4- Elohim, God Our Creator- Genesis 1:1

The very first sentence in The Bible tells you, *"In the beginning, God created the heavens and the earth"* (Genesis 1:1, NLT). The name Elohim is a plural noun and comes from two root words—*"El" meaning strength and unlimited power* and the rest stands for *"allah" meaning "The God"* coming from a contraction Arabic phrase. Together, this says, **The God of Strength and Unlimited Power.** Because God is The Creator, there is nothing here on earth, under the earth, or in the heavens that was not made by Him or came from something He created. Therefore, you have faith in Him and who you are, as His creation, in His image and His likeness. *As He Is, So Are you— You are a Creator too!*

What scripture(s) speaks to you that God is the Creator of all things and The God of Strength and Unlimited Power? Write it/them out below.

5- El Chay ("Chey"), The Living God- Jeremiah 10:10a

"But the Lord is the only True God. He is the Living God and the Everlasting King," (Jeremiah 10:10a, NLT). Your God is Real and He is Powerful! He is the ONLY TRUE LIVING GOD! When you grasp this concept and KNOW without a shadow of a doubt this truth, you no longer have a desire to put any other gods before Him. You no longer give life to false gods—false image of yourself, other people, money system, career, houses, vehicles, etc.). The Almighty God is your life sustainer, and your faith lies in Him alone.

What scripture(s) lets you know that God is The True and Living God? Write it/them out below.

_____
_____
_____
_____
_____
_____
_____
_____
_____
_____
_____
_____
_____

_____

_____

_____

_____

_____

_____

_____

_____

As I stated before, these are merely a FEW of the names of God that describe His Character. I encourage you to seek out more on the Names of God—God The Father, God The Son, and God The Holy Spirit—and use references included in the back of this manual.

These Names of God tells you (or reminds you) that you have faith in your God Who:

- **SEES ALL (El Roi)**
- **IS EVERYWHERE (Jehovah-Shammah)**
- **IS THE BEGINNING and THE END, (Alpha and Omega)**
- **IS CREATOR OF EVERYTHING (ELOHIM)**
- **IS THE LIVING GOD (EL CHAY)**

Since God is ALL THESE THINGS AND MORE—you *should* have no problem having faith in Him and His Word! He sees and knows everything about you and all things concerning you; there is nowhere you can find yourself and God isn't there, because He is at the beginning of it, He is at the end of it, and He is there during the process of it; because He created everything, He knows everything about it all, and that is because He is alive and well! Come on now! Reading Hebrews, Chapter 11, *"NOW FAITH IS..."* should give you a whole new meaning! You will be able to *test it and see*!

Your Work

Write down some scriptures about faith that you can SPEAK into your atmosphere and over your life.

_____
_____
_____
_____
_____
_____
_____
_____
_____
_____
_____
_____

The names mentioned above are a starting point and helps you learn more about how God's character forms the foundation of your faith mindset. As you come to know Him even deeper through His names, your mindset of faith is built on the understanding that you serve a God who is powerful, present, eternal, and intimately involved in your life.

NOTES

4
Let's Sum It Up

The initial three chapters establish a comprehensive framework for understanding faith. Faith is presented not solely as a belief but as a life-altering force that influences your thoughts, actions, and relationship with God.

In **Chapter 1**, you explored *what faith truly is*, distinguishing it from mere belief. While belief acknowledges truth, faith requires action—belief clings, but faith lets go. It is not simply mental agreement; it is trust in motion, a surrender that allows God to move in your life. An examination of how your *beliefs form a belief system* was conducted, shaping your thought patterns and responses to life. Many people operate within inherited or conditioned belief systems that limit their faith. To walk in bold faith, one must *rewire the mind*—tearing down limiting beliefs and rebuilding a new faith system aligned with God's Word. This process involves deep self-examination to unlearn doubt and embrace a renewed perspective that reflects God and Who He is. The incorruptible seed of God's Word was discussed, and you found that as a seed carries within it the substance of life, your faith produces faith (life) within you. The incorruptible seed is the source of your spiritual rebirth and transformation.

Chapter 2 delves into *the power of bold faith* and its connection to mindset. You learned that faith isn't a feeling; it is a disciplined decision. In this chapter, you walked through the Hall of Faith with it's champions in Hebrews Chapter 11. It gave a vivid picture of their stories which went beyond just believing but demonstrated faith as a vibrant force that drives obedience, courage, and perseverance. The analysis of this chapter in Hebrews, explored how faith manifests in practical ways and how it should shape your purpose and trust in God. This illustration gave you the ability to see when faith is actively lived out, it will become the groundwork for fulfilling God's Plan and advancing His Kingdom.

Chapter 3 introduces *five meanings and names of God*, showing how His character is revealed through His names. Understanding the nature of God—*Jehovah-Shammah, Alpha and Omega, Elohim, El Roi, and EL Chay*—allows you to deepen your trust and align your faith with His divine nature. You received the concept that your faith mindset is grounded in the Character of God, how He sees you, how you see yourself, and how you see the world around you. Because faith goes beyond intellectual agreement, it calls you to trust in God's character—His goodness, faithfulness, and sovereignty. When you know who God is, your faith is unmovable; it is rooted in the unchanging character of God Himself.

Together, these chapters laid the groundwork for shifting from passive belief to an active faith system rooted in the unchanging character of God.

The foundational truths that have been established thus far have created a divine revelation that will now allow you to receive the next concepts: Understanding the Mind of God and how it regenerates the Mind of Man. You will learn the difference between self-consciousness and God-consciousness and how shifting your perspective to align with God's truth transforms your faith walk. As you journey through these next chapters, you will see how the mind and the brain work together, how a regenerated mindset is essential for spiritual growth, and ultimately, how love is the all-conclusive determinant of the mindset of faith. This progression will help guide you to a deeper connection with God and His Word, allowing His wisdom to become your wisdom. Let this be your motivation to shape your thoughts and actions according to His Word and unfalteringly lead you to His divinely orchestrated purpose for your life.

NOTES

NOTES

5

How the Brain and Mind Work Together

Key Terms

Illumination of The Spirit – The process by which the Holy Spirit brings clarity, revelation, and spiritual understanding to God's sons.

Mind – The inner faculty of thought, reasoning, and belief where decisions are made and spiritual understanding is formed.

Spirit of God – Another name for the Holy Spirit, representing God's presence, power, and personality at work in the earth and in His sons.

Spirit-Revealed Words – Words spoken under the guidance and revelation of the Holy Spirit.

The Enlightened Knowledge of The Spirit – The deep, divine insight that comes from a Spirit-led understanding of God's Word and nature.

Now, I will be the first to say, I am no psychologist (A person who studies the mind and how it works). During my undergraduate and postgraduate studies in communication, I have gained knowledge, conducted research, and attended courses on various related topics. I use this educational background and my new research processes here to explore and discuss how the brain and the mind work. I will get a bit technical but will break it down for the importance of the topic to be clearly understood and how it correlates with faith. Let's dive in.

Before starting my research on this topic, the Holy Spirit gave me an inclination that there is a difference between the human brain and the mind. During this process, the following is some of the information I gathered.

The Human Brain

The following information is my research conducted to help explain the function of the brain at the primary educational level. This helps put it into practical terms for better understanding and clarity.

"The brain is a complex organ that controls thought, memory, emotion, touch, motor skills, vision, breathing, temperature, hunger and every process

that regulates our body. Together, the brain and spinal cord that extends from it make up the central nervous system, or CNS.

The brain sends and receives chemical and electrical signals (messages) throughout the body. Different signals control different processes, and your brain interprets each. Some make you feel tired, for example, while others make you feel pain.

Some messages are kept within the brain, while others are relayed through the spine and across the body's vast network of nerves to distant extremities. To do this, the central nervous system relies on billions of neurons (nerve cells), (www.hopkinsmedicine.org, 2024).

"We use our brains constantly for a variety of activities that, while crucial to our survival, require no conscious thought. For instance, the human brain is responsible for involuntary activities, such as regulating heartbeat, breathing, and blinking. Although the brain controls both voluntary and involuntary activities, different regions of the brain are devoted to each type of task.

The brain changes throughout life. Although lots of changes happen while it grows during embryonic development and early life, scientists have discovered that changes in the brain are not restricted to early life. Even in the adult brain, neurons continue to form new connections, strengthen existing connections, or eliminate connections as we continue to learn. Recent studies have shown that some neurons in the adult brain retain the ability to divide. Finally, damaged neurons have some capability to regenerate if the conditions are right" (NIH, The National Library of Medicine, 2007).

So then, the brain can be referred to as the physical, tangible, human organ that is a vital part of how our entire body functions. It is the "Command Center" of your physical body, and it is constantly processing data from the outside world, and from within. The brain is inputting the information from the five senses—seeing, hearing, tasting, touching, smelling—and is considered to be the "hardware" that processes this sensory input. It represents the "human side" of who you are.

The Mind

Key Terms

Interdependence of the mind and brain – The dynamic and mutual relationship between the mind and the brain.

Reactive (Reaction) – Acting quickly and impulsively from emotion or habit, without spiritual discernment.

Responsive (Respond) – Making thoughtful, spirit-led decisions based on God's truth and a renewed mind.

In essence, your **mind** is *the inner faculty of thought, reasoning, and belief where decisions are made, and spiritual understanding is formed.* It is the bridge between the soul and spirit, shaping how you perceive and respond to both God and the world. It is the "software" and processes information through a complex series of cognitive functions that involve receiving, interpreting, storing, and responding (providing output) to various forms of input, (the five senses) and produces your rational thinking. As part of this process, emotions play a significant role in how the mind processes information. Emotional responses can shape how we perceive, interpret, and store this information. During this process, the information collected through the mind (created by its perception and attention), encodes the information into memory—short term and long term. The brain then organizes and helps to interpret this information based on existing knowledge and experiences (stored in short or long-term memory).

Then finally, the mind provides the decision-making part of the process by responding to the input it received. This is accomplished when the mind uses all the processed information—sensory input, memories, and emotions—to make decisions and guide behavior. This decision-making process can be quick and intuitive, as reflexive actions happens automatically— as in a **reaction**; or the process can be slow and deliberate—when you weigh pros and cons to solve a complex problem—as in a **response**.

Although these processes exist simultaneously as in concert (the natural and spiritual **interdependence of the mind and brain**), there is still a debate on this miraculous phenomenon: The Argument of the Mind-Brain Problem.

The Argument of the Mind-Brain Problem

There is a "problem" that exists in the neuroscience world that states:

"Because the brain is a physical organ that can be measured, observed and analyzed (objective in nature), and the mind is the intangible part of the human thought processes, and is individual and personal (subjective in nature), it cannot be measured and studied to the degree that the brain can be. Humans disagree on its existence of being two separate entities, or being two in one that are interdependent upon the other" (Barrett, 2009).

Despite this human debate, this is what I received from the Holy Spirit:

"The reason that this problem exists is because everyone (up to this point) that has studied this phenomenon does not have the knowledge of the spiritual man, so they cannot agree whether the mind and brain are the same or are they different." But because of the Word of God, we know that it is NOT the same, and it is the MIND that is renewed in Christ, and not the brain. ***So, the brain is how your physical being processes what your spiritual consciousness perceives.***

Because God created you—He manufactured HIMSELF into you—He knows everything about what He made. HE IS THE

CREATOR! So, God knew your physical brain could not grasp His spiritual nature on its own, that's why your mind is so important and discussed in the bible, and not the brain!

Now, let's look at some bible scriptures that explain this a little more.

Mark 12:30 (NIV) *And you shall love the Lord your God with all your heart and with all your soul and* **with all your mind** *and with all your strength.*

Notice, you can't love God with your brain—its your mind that understands the concept of love. Your brain just processes the input you give it.

Isaiah 26:3 (English Standard Version—ESV) *You keep him in perfect peace whose* **mind** *is stayed on You, because he trusts in You.*

Your mind is where God dwells, not your brain. So, where He is, there is peace.

Romans 7:25b (TPT) *So if left to myself, the flesh is aligned with the law of sin, but now my* **renewed mind** *is fixed on and submitted to God's righteous principles.*

It's your MIND that let's you focus and submit to God's way of doing things; your brain just obeys what the Nature of God guides it to. Once you submit to His will, your body aligns with the spirit of who you are.

Romans 12:2 (ESV) *Do not be conformed to this world, but be transformed by the* **renewal of your mind** *that by testing you may discern what is the will of God; what is good and acceptable and perfect.*

Again, the renewing of your mind is what transforms you. It causes a change to occur in your inward being, that can then be seen on your outer being. This also tells you that it is through your mind that you can discern what God's will is for you. I LOVE how the Passion Translation says it: **"Stop imitating the ideas and opinions of the culture around you, but be inwardly transformed by the Holy Spirit through a total reformation of how you think. This will empower you to discern God's will as you live a beautiful life, satisfying and perfect in His eyes"**. Oh, My, GOD!!! Is that not beautifully written? You are being told by Apostle Paul (the author of this book in the bible), that if you are to be like Christ, you cannot be influenced by or model your life by pop culture and what it stands for! He knows it's because of your human nature (sin), that causes you to naturally gravitate towards it. But if you want to be in the perfect will of God (that is pass His good and acceptable will), YOUR MIND MUST BE TOTALLY TRANSFORMED!

Key Terms

God's Divine Nature – The essence of who God is—perfect in love, righteousness, justice, holiness, and power.

God's Grace – The unearned, undeserved favor and kindness of God extended toward humanity.

Holy Spirit – The third person of the Trinity (The Father -God; The Son -Jesus Christ; and The Holy Spirit -God's Spirit).

Illumination of The Spirit – The process by which the Holy Spirit brings clarity, revelation, and spiritual understanding.

Renewed Mind / Renewal of the Mind – The transformation of the mind to align with God's truth through the power of the Holy Spirit.

Spirit-Revealed Words – Words spoken under the guidance and revelation of the Holy Spirit. They carry power, divine authority, and clarity beyond human reasoning, often bringing breakthrough, healing, and understanding.

The Enlightened Knowledge of The Spirit – The deep, divine insight that comes from a Spirit-led understanding of God's Word and nature. It goes beyond facts and logic, producing wisdom, transformation, and intimacy with God.

Foundational passage of scripture

The following verses are your second foundational scriptures that this training manual explores:

1 Corinthians 2:11-15 (TPT) *After all, who can really see into a person's heart and know his hidden impulses except for that person's spirit? So, it is*

with God. *His thoughts and secrets are only fully understood by His Spirit—The Spirit of God. For we did not receive the spirit of this world system but the Spirit of God, so that we might come to understand and experience all that grace has lavished upon us. And we articulate these realities with the words imparted to us by The Spirit and not with the words taught by human wisdom. We join together Spirit Revealed Truths with Spirit Revealed Words. Someone living on an entirely human level rejects the revelations of God's Spirit, for they make no sense to him. He can't understand the revelations of The Spirit because they are only discovered by the illumination of The Spirit. Those who live in The Spirit are able to carefully evaluate all things; and they are subject to the scrutiny of no one but God.*

The revelation that God gave me for this is: *Spirit Revealed Truths are The Word of God; and Spirit Revealed Words, are the Words of God you speak out loud! Because The Spirit revealed those words to you. You can only comprehend these revelations (of the Spirit) when God's Word is illuminated (to make something visible or bright by shining a light on it; help to clarify or explain) in you.*

That's it in a nutshell! This gives a picture of how the mind (your renewed intellect of God's Spirit) and the brain (your natural intellect) works. Now, look at the break down—line upon line, percept upon percept.

1. ***After all, who can really see into a person's heart and know his hidden impulses except for that person's spirit? So, it is with God. His thoughts and secrets are***

only fully understood by His Spirit—The Spirit of God. This explains what was shared earlier about the mind being an individual entity for each person. Everyone's mind works differently because of their personal experiences and how they perceive and interpret those experiences. And the same is true of God. You can only experience Him, through The Spirit of who He is—not your own human experiences—but by the knowledge and understanding of God through His Word.

2. *For we did not receive the spirit of this world system but the Spirit of God, so that we might come to understand and experience all that grace has lavished upon us.* When you were first *created* in the Mind of God, you borne (carried) His Spirit. However, once you entered into the earth realm (through natural birth), you were separated from God's Spirit and then took on human spirit only. Once you were "born again"—repentance, forgiveness of your sins, and living a new, better life—you should no longer operate by the world system (and its way of doing things). Because God gave you His Spirit, you can better understand His **grace (God's undeserved and unmerited favor)** that He pours over you! So, having God's Spirit (His Mind and way of doing things), helps you understand Him and His ways.

3. *And we articulate these realities with the words imparted to us by The Spirit and not with the words taught by human wisdom. We join together Spirit Revealed Truths with Spirit Revealed Words.* There

is no other way to express the realities of **God's Divine Nature** (His Spirit Revealed Truths in His Word) than to allow the **Holy Spirit** to speak *to you* (As God's renewed son) and *through you* with Spirit Revealed Words (you speaking God's Word). Your language, along with your mind, has been renewed and changed, therefore, when you speak Spirit Revealed Words, they come from God's Spirit and not what your natural mind and the world around you has taught you.

4. *Someone living on an entirely human level rejects the revelations of God's Spirit, for they make no sense to him. He can't understand the revelations of The Spirit because they are only discovered by the illumination of The Spirit.* Someone that limits their experience of God being in their life at the human level (the natural, physical state of being), cannot understand or grasp the revelation of Spirit Revealed Truths. The mind of man and its thought processes cannot compute these and must first be renewed so that it can discover (perceive) God-given understanding through **the enlightened knowledge of the Spirit** (of God).

5. *Those who live in The Spirit are able to carefully evaluate all things; and they are subject to the scrutiny of no one but God.* Living in The Spirit (of God) is the only way to have the capability of assessing all things pertaining to life—natural life and spiritual life. That means, if you truly live by God's Spirit dwelling inside you,

God is the one that will conduct the examination/evaluation.

How it all comes together

This chapter carried a lot of concepts about the natural and spiritual side of who you are. Now, let's look at how it all works together when it comes to your faith:

Faith is not just a spiritual concept—it is deeply connected to how the mind and brain function together. The brain processes information: it stores memory, triggers emotions, and controls physical responses. But the mind is where reasoning, decision-making, and belief systems live. Faith operates in the mind, because that is where choices are made—especially the decision to believe God beyond what is seen, felt, or understood in the natural.

While the brain receives input from the world, it is the mind that filters that input through either a faith-based lens or a fear-based one. The **renewed mind**—one that has been transformed by the Word and Spirit of God—learns to override old thought patterns that are wired for survival, doubt, or control. Instead, it aligns with Spirit-Revealed Truths, allowing God's sons to respond in faith rather than fear.

When faith is active, the mind begins to govern the brain's reactions, training it to support spiritual truth rather than merely reacting to natural circumstances. For example, when the world says "impossible," a faith-filled mind, informed by God's Word, tells the brain "With God, all things are possible" (Matthew 19:26 NIV). This creates new neural pathways—literally rewiring the brain to believe and act on faith-based thinking.

In short, the mind chooses faith, and over time, the brain learns to support that decision through consistency, renewal, and practice. Faith is not a denial of what the brain sees or feels—it is a conscious, intentional decision of the mind to trust God above all and train every part of the self to agree with His Word.

Your Work

What are some scriptures that you have found that demonstrate how your thoughts and mind should be governed in a renewed, restored state?

_____
_____
_____
_____
_____
_____
_____
_____
_____
_____
_____
_____
_____
_____
_____
_____
_____
_____
_____
_____

How will you use these to make better decisions for your everyday life?

6

The Regenerated Mind(set)

Key Terms

Divine Knowledge – Spiritual understanding and truth that comes directly from God.

Regenerated Mind (The Mind Rewire Process) – The transformation that takes place when the human mind is renewed by God's Spirit and Word.

The topic of the **regenerated mind** is one that can also be complex, while at the same time very enlightening for learning about the Mindset of Faith. Understanding the difference between your brain and your mind, then how you are to "rewire" it to a state of renewal is necessary in making "The Change" and "Doing the Work" needed for the change. This is what the regenerated mind is— **The Mind Rewire Process.** Let's now look at what a regenerated mindset is, and how it comes into play.

What is Regenerated?

It is important here to break down some definitions. First, a look at the natural meaning of the word **regenerated,** then the spiritual meaning of it.

When looking up the word, I found the word regeneration. The prefix *re-* means "again". Generation means "to produce offspring" or "cause to be born". Together, **regeneration** means, *to be born again, or that which is born again*— this is the natural meaning. The spiritual meaning is *the impartation of a new and divine life, a new creation; the production of a new thing.* It is not a change in your old nature (mindset), it is the creation of a TOTALLY, new nature (new mindset). This new nature (mindset) is given to you by God (Created in His Image, 1988).

My apostle and spiritual mentor, taught it like this: *You must be RE-GENED; you must have the DNA of God and be re-wired to the Standard of Heaven* (Z. Legette, 2024). That means when you take on your TRUE identity, you walk in faith and act like your daddy (Father God)! You talk like Him, walk like Him, and look like

Him! That's what getting a new mindset is—*Reconnecting to God and HIS Gene.*

Just as your biological DNA determines your physical traits, your spiritual DNA—God's **D**ownloaded **N**ature **A**ctivated (J. Hardin-Gautier, 2024) —shapes your identity in Him. When you reconnect with God, His divine nature overrides the limitations of your human nature, transforming how you think, believe, and operate. This leads to the next essential concept: Understanding what a mindset is and how it influences your faith journey.

What is a Mindset?

Key Terms

Divine Knowledge – Spiritual understanding and truth that comes directly from God.

Fixed Mindset – The belief that abilities, intelligence, and talents are static and unchangeable.

Growth Mindset – The belief that skills, knowledge, and intelligence can be developed through dedication, learning, and effort.

Neuroplasticity – The brain's ability to reorganize itself by forming new neural connections throughout life.

Word Utterance – A spoken word, statement, or vocal sound. In the spiritual context, utterances—especially when Spirit-led—carry divine weight.

Mindset *is a set of attitudes, beliefs, and thought patterns that influence how a person perceives and responds to situations. It shapes behavior, decision-making, and how one approaches challenges or opportunities.*

The mind and the process of creating a new mindset work together through a combination of cognitive flexibility, intentional thought patterns, and **neuroplasticity,** which is *the* *brain's ability to reorganize itself.* A new mindset can be developed by consciously reshaping the way you think, perceive, and respond to the world. Here's how this process unfolds:

1. The mind encompasses your thoughts, beliefs, perceptions, and emotions. It interprets reality based on past experiences, current beliefs, and ongoing thoughts. These patterns create your mindset. There are two types of mindsets: **Fixed Mindset** and **Growth Mindset**. A ***fixed mindset*** *puts limitations on your abilities and sees it as stagnant, while a* **growth mindset** *adapts the concept of being fluid with the ability to change and develop due to your <u>efforts</u> made over time.* These are the natural definitions. The spiritual meaning for this has to do with *the <u>"effort"</u> that is produced and must come through acting on your faith.* Because of the **divine knowledge** *given by Spirit Revealed Truths, you can act upon them as a part of the mind renewing process.*

2. *A fixed mindset* can create limited beliefs keeping you stuck in negative thought patterns *(contrary to God's Word and the life He has for you)*, while empowering beliefs *(growth mindset with Spirit Revealed Truths)* allows you to embrace growth, change, and God-Inspired Renewal.

3. When you adopt *new* thought patterns or behaviors, your brain rewires itself to support this new way of thinking *(neuroplasticity)*. This process helps your brain to form new connections and reorganizes itself in response to *new*

thoughts and *new* learning, that leads to *new* experiences. The Holy Spirit provides clarity to me here: *"When you act upon your faith, your natural brain rewires and reorganizes itself and responds in a new and different way; from which you encounter new experiences. This is after you activate Spirit Revealed Truths by your acts of faith and speaking Spirit Revealed Words".* Romans 10:17 in the TPT says this, "Faith, then, is birthed in a heart that responds to God's anointed utterance of the Anointed One." The meaning of the word **utterance** *is a spoken word, statement, or vocal sound.* This means that once you receive God's Spirit Revealed Truths (His Word), you activate your faith by speaking His Word, making bold statements of His Word, and releasing vocal sounds that represent His Word into your atmosphere, causing you to have a new experience each time you activate it.

Creating a New Mindset

Creating a new mindset involves intentionally changing your thought patterns and beliefs. Here's how the mind and brain collaborate in this process:

1. Awareness of Current Beliefs

The first step in creating a new mindset is becoming aware of your current thoughts and beliefs. The mind tends to follow established patterns that reinforce old mindsets. By bringing awareness to these thoughts, you can begin to identify which beliefs serve you and which limit your growth.

Your Work:

How can limited mindset beliefs keep you from having a renewed mind? What scriptures can help in this renewal process?

_____
_____
_____
_____
_____
_____
_____
_____
_____
_____
_____
_____
_____
_____
_____
_____
_____
_____
_____

2. Challenging Limiting Beliefs

Once you've identified limiting beliefs, the mind can actively challenge them. This involves questioning the validity of these beliefs and replacing them with new, empowering ones. For instance, instead of thinking, "I always fail," you challenge that belief with evidence of past successes *AND replacing that thought with the Spirit Revealed Truth that, "God has unveiled His unlimited riches and favor within you, and He floods your innermost being with supernatural strength" (Ephesians 3:16-TPT, paraphased).* This process helps to weaken the old belief (old mindset) and build a foundation for a new mindset.

Your Work:

What are some ways to challenge and replace your old mindset? Include some scriptures that reinforce this.

_____
_____
_____
_____
_____
_____
_____
_____
_____
_____
_____
_____
_____
_____
_____
_____
_____
_____
_____
_____

3. **Start the brain rewire process**

To rewire the brain, you need to consistently practice new thought patterns. Repetition is key to strengthening (neural) connections. *Declarations of God's Word*, visualization, and reframing negative thoughts assists to recondition the mind. For example, *speaking the Word of God into your atmosphere, disrupts current activity and creates a more conducive environment* to visualize yourself successful, overcoming challenges, and reinforcing a growth mindset. *This builds expectation for the Spirit Revealed Truth to become your reality.*

Your Work:

What are some declarations of God's Word you can use to reinforce your growth mindset?

_____
_____
_____
_____
_____
_____
_____
_____
_____

_____

_____

_____

_____

_____

_____

_____

_____

_____

4. Taking Action to Reinforce New Beliefs *(Faith in Action)*

The bible states in James 2:26, *"For just as the body without the spirit is dead, so also faith without works is dead"* (New American Standard Bible, NASB). Therefore, faith requires action. When you take action, it solidifies the connection between the brain and the new mindset. When you take steps aligned with your new beliefs, you confirm them in your brain (your processing center). For example, if your new mindset involves believing you can improve your skills, you reinforce that belief *by actually practicing and developing those skills.* As your actions align with your new mindset, it becomes more deeply ingrained. Reading and getting understanding of God's Word—with Holy Spirit inspiration—The Words of the Bible become your SPIRIT REVEALED TRUTHS! *It is not possible to get the FULL TRUTH, without first the desire to know the truth. This helps to also build and grow your faith.* As you build and grow your faith, you start to develop a *God-Consciousness and leave self-consciousness behind.* This is our next topic. But first, finish your work below.

Your Work:

What are some actions you will take to align with your new mindset?

_____
_____
_____
_____
_____
_____
_____
_____
_____
_____
_____
_____
_____
_____
_____
_____

NOTES

7
Faith Requires God-Consciousness

Key Terms

God-Consciousness – The spiritual awareness and continual acknowledgment of God's presence, character, and will.

Self-Consciousness – A heightened awareness of oneself, especially in how one is perceived or judged by others or even oneself.

Wisdom – In the biblical sense, it is the knowledge of God's divine plan, especially truths that were once hidden but are now revealed through His Spirit.

The maturing of your faith is how you move from being a b*eliever to being a son.* This means you graduate from believing the Word of God, to *being* The Word of God. This transformation can only come when you develop **God-Consciousness** in your life. The shift is about operating from His level of thinking, aligning your thoughts with His truth, and trusting in His power rather than your own human limitations. Too often, self-consciousness—your fears, doubts, and past experiences—are allowed to shape your decisions and restrict your faith. But true faith requires something greater: a renewed mind that is fully aware of God's presence, power, and purpose in your life.

Let's look at what it means to transition from self-consciousness to God-consciousness and how this change is essential for walking in bold, unwavering faith.

What is Self-Consciousness vs. God-Consciousness?

Society talks a lot about being self-aware and understanding ourselves so that we can know how we operate and function with the world around us. They put lots of focus on self and things that motivates "the self". Therefore, **s***elf-consciousness is the heightened awareness of oneself, particularly in relation to how others may perceive or judge you, including yourself.* It often involves a focus on personal appearance, behavior, or actions, and can lead to feelings of awkwardness, insecurity, or embarrassment. While it can encourage self-reflection, excessive self-consciousness can result in anxiety and social discomfort, making it difficult to act naturally in social situations.

When you focus on self too much, you have limited ability to operate from your *full intended state*. Being self-conscious is like functioning with an imbalance. Too much of "self" diminishes The Spirit Revealed Truths of who you fully are. You are not only self (body, mind, and emotions), but you are spirit. And it is through that spirit that you become God-Conscious. This is when Spirit Revealed Truths become fused with your spirit—and reveal the truth of who you are. These truths now resonate in you, and not the lies of the enemy. *God wants you to be self-aware through Him,* which leads to being ever aware of Him in you. When you are aware (take notice) of yourself in this way, you realize you are a son of God.

Therefore, being *God Conscious is the spiritual awareness of God's Presence (His Glory), Character (Who He is), and His Will (His Purpose/Plan)*. Because it is more than just acknowledging God's existence, it requires you to totally submerge yourself in His glory, having revelation of who He is, and living in alignment with His purpose. This consciousness transforms the mind and creates an atmosphere for your faith to be activated. When you develop a mind that is God-Conscious, you can then rise above fear, doubt, and worldly distractions around you, living a life of clarity, peace, and success in whatever you do, because you have The Mind of God.

There are several scriptures that talks about your mind and helping you to be more God-Conscious—here are a few: (Some are mentioned previously.)

Romans 12:2 (NIV): *"Do not conform to the pattern of this world, but be transformed by the renewing of your mind. Then you will be able to test and approve what God's will is—His good, pleasing, and perfect will."*

This verse highlights the life-altering power of God Consciousness. Renewing the mind involves letting go of worldly perspectives and adopting God's Spirit-Revealed Truths. Faith thrives when the mind aligns with God's Divine Nature and His Way of doing things, enabling His sons to discern His will in every situation.

Philippians 2:5 (NKJV): "Let this mind be in you which was also in Christ Jesus."

Adopting the mind of Christ requires humility, obedience, and love. When your thoughts reflect His, faith is strengthened, and actions are guided by His higher purpose. This mindset fosters determination to trust in God and His plan.

Isaiah 26:3 (NIV): *"You will keep in perfect peace those whose minds are steadfast, because they trust in You."*

A steadfast mind, rooted in God-Consciousness, creates a foundation of peace and faith. Trusting in God allows you to navigate challenges without fear, knowing that faith anchors you in divine protection.

2 Corinthians 10:5 (NIV): *"We demolish arguments and every pretension that sets itself up against the knowledge of God, and we take captive every thought to make it obedient to Christ."*

This verse emphasizes the importance of controlling your thoughts. A mind focused on God rejects negativity, doubt, and fear, creating space for faith to flourish.

For the next scripture reference, I had to share how The Passion Translation says it:

Colossians 3:2 (TPT): "Yes, feast on all the *treasures of the heavenly realm* and fill your thoughts with heavenly realities, and not with the distractions of the natural realm."

To have a mindset that comes from the heavenly realm is to have God-Consciousness. His thoughts are always higher than your natural thoughts (from the natural realm). When your mind is God-Conscious, you prioritize God's kingdom, and your decisions and perspectives align with His purpose. You are no longer distracted by what is going on around you, and you can partake of all that God has for you—His Fullness!

Your Work:

How can you become (more) God-Conscious versus self-conscious?

What new practice(s) will you implement to allow your God-Consciousness to help develop your faith?

_____
_____
_____
_____
_____
_____
_____
_____
_____
_____
_____
_____
_____
_____
_____
_____
_____
_____
_____
_____

The Mind of God (God-Consciousness) IS the Mindset of Faith

To have the "Mind of God" is to view the world through His Word and His character. It transforms how you see and process adversity, shifting your focus from yourself and your natural way of seeing and doing things, to the vastness of your Great Almighty God, and the power He has given you to operate in. *When your mind is saturated with God's Word, your faith becomes a natural response to life's challenges.* You can declare, like Jesus taught His disciples, *"...say to this mountain, move away from here and go over there, and you will see it move! There is nothing you can't do!" (Matthew 17:20b, TPT).* This happens when your confidence is grounded, not in your natural abilities, but in God's supernatural power working in and through you!

As God's son on the earth, you are to live in this place of being conscious of Him every day and in every way! Doing so brings your thoughts, your mind, and actions into alignment with God's very own heart and what He wants for you. *When you are God-Conscious, all things that were once unknown and a mystery to you, are then revealed.* This takes you back FULL CIRCLE—to First Corinthians, chapter two:

Verses 6-7: *However, there is a wisdom that we continually speak of when we are among the spiritually mature. It's wisdom that didn't originate in this present age, nor did it come from the rulers of this age who are in the process of being dethroned. Instead, we continually speak of this wonderful wisdom that comes from God, hidden before now in a mystery. It is His secret plan destined before the ages to bring us into glory (TPT).*

Let's dissect this and give the foundation of it. First, Paul started in verse one, explaining to the church in Corinth that although he was well versed in theology of man (knowledge of Jewish laws and The Hebrew Bible), he wanted his message to be clear and singularly focused: He wanted to share the Mind of God through the Life of Christ Jesus. Then he continues in verse six saying:

(Paraphrased) *Despite this, there is a language we use when we are communicating with those who are "spiritually mature"*—meaning those who have God's Mind and a Mindset of Faith. (Because they believed God's Word when they received it). This tells you that, *to have God's Mind (His thoughts and way of doing things), you must be spiritually mature and have faith in what He has said (to you and about you).* If you want to have God's Mind and be God-Conscious, YOU MUST BE SPIRITUALLY MATURE.

In the Amplified Bible, it breaks it down even further: verse six- "Yet, when we are among the full-grown (spiritually mature Christians who are ripe in understanding), we do impart a [higher] **wisdom (knowledge of the divine plan previously hidden)**; but it is indeed not a wisdom of this present age or of this world, nor of the leaders and rulers of this age..."

Paul is simply saying, the type of wisdom he is talking about is not of this world. No philosophers, theologians, or any others with earthly knowledge and wisdom understand it—but ANYONE who has received the Mindset of God (Faith Mindset) understands His mysteries, and they are no longer hidden to them.

Verse 7b goes on to say: "It is His secret plan, destined before the ages, to bring us into glory".

The word **"glory"** (a noun- representing a person, a place, or a thing), can be translated as glorification (a verb- a word of action). **Glorification** means, *the act of giving glory or honor to someone or something. It is the act of praising or exalting someone or something to a high degree; the act of recognizing and celebrating the greatness or excellence of a person or thing; refers to the process of* ***being elevated to a higher spiritual state.***

This does not mean you are better than others in the nature sense. God has created us all equal, in His likeness and in His image. However, just as in the military, educational circles, and the like, there are levels and ranks of position. When you have the Mind of God, and operate from that place in your life, you live from an elevated spiritual state of being. This scripture is letting you know, **God wants you to know Him**; There is nothing he wants hidden from you, because He has fully revealed Himself to you through Christ Jesus. So, when you are full-grown and spiritually mature, the Holy Spirit can **bring you into glory (allow His Greatness and Excellence in you to be seen).** Simply put, God celebrates His Greatness in you—AND YOU SHOULD TOO! Once you experience this higher degree of life, understanding The Mind of God and His Way of doing things, and activating it in your life—this is **The Mindset of Faith!**

Your Work:

How can your Mindset of Faith help you respond to life's challenges?

_____

_____

_____

_____

_____

_____

_____

_____

_____

_____

_____

_____

_____

_____

_____

_____

What does being "Spiritually Mature" mean to you?

What are some ways you can celebrate God's Greatness in you on a daily basis?

_____
_____
_____
_____
_____
_____
_____
_____
_____
_____
_____
_____
_____
_____
_____
_____
_____
_____

How will you implement Your Mindset of Faith?

NOTES

8

The Conclusion of the Matter is LOVE

Key Terms

Natural (Human) Love – In the natural or human context, love is often based on emotions, attraction, personal connection, or conditions.

Spiritual (Godly) Love – Spiritually, love is unconditional, sacrificial, and rooted in God's nature. It's not based on feelings or conditions but on truth, grace, and purpose.

Throughout this journey of developing a Mindset of Faith, you have explored the foundational truths of faith, how it shapes your thoughts, and the transformation that occurs when you shift from self-consciousness to God-consciousness. Now, we arrive at the ultimate revelation—*love is the glue that holds a faith mindset together.*

Because of the emotional context that is usually associated with the word, **"love"**, it can sometimes be limited to the human level of its experience. But love is truly the essence of who God is. It is the very force that activates and sustains faith. Without love, faith is empty, unstable, and ineffective. But when faith is rooted in love, it becomes constant, life-changing, and is aligned with God's divine nature.

Here's how **love solidifies the faith mindset:**

- **Love is the Foundation of Faith** – Faith is powered by love; without it, faith lacks substance and effectiveness. Love strengthens and sustains a life of unwavering faith.

- **Love Renews the Mindset** – Faith rooted in love reshapes thoughts, attitudes, and actions, aligning them with God's truth instead of fear, doubt, or worldly influences.

- **Love Creates Unity and Strength** – Love deepens connection with God and others, reinforcing confidence in His Word and cultivating bold, steadfast faith.

- **Love Drives Spiritual Maturity** – As a son of God, you grow in God-Consciousness and love fuels your transformation, ensuring faith evolves beyond belief into an active, Spirit-filled experience.

- **Love Grounds Faith in God's Nature** – Because God is love, a faith mindset built on love remains firm, providing stability, fortitude, and assurance in every season of life.

This scripture describes it clearly:

Ephesians 3: 17-19 (TPT) *"Then by constantly using your faith, the life of Christ will be released deep inside you, and the resting place of HIS LOVE will become the very source and root of your life. Then you will be empowered to discover what every holy one experiences—the great magnitude of the astonishing LOVE of Christ in all its dimensions. How deeply intimate and far-reaching is His LOVE! How enduring and inclusive it is! Endless LOVE beyond measurement that transcends our understanding—this extravagant LOVE pours into you until you are filled to overflowing with the fullness of God!"*

The bible emphasizes the importance of the word "love" with it being mentioned over 466 times and up to 759 times in the bible, depending on the bible translation and the word's variations, (e.g., NIV, KJV, ESV, TPT). It is a central theme in the epistle of Ephesians, as Apostle Paul emphasizes God's love for humanity, the love God's sons should have for one another, and the role of love in living your life with Christ. The chapter in the bible that most people know as the "Love Chapter" is 1 Corinthians 13. When I read it again in the TPT, I received a new revelation of the true significance of love in my life. The title of it in this bible translation is, *"Love, The Motivation of Our Lives"*, and the chapter reveals what love IS, and what IT IS NOT. In its totality, love is ranked above spiritual gifts and human works;

everything you do must be rooted in love. Love is also required to overcome negative emotions such as jealousy, offense, failure, and shame. The last verses of the chapter are titled, *"Perfect Love"*, and this is where you find out the *conclusion of the matter:*

It is interesting that the Apostle Paul (the writer) in this chapter mentions that when he was a child, he spoke, reasoned, and saw things as a child; but when he matured, he set aside his childish ways. This leads to the understanding that it takes maturity to live at this level of faith, that love truly conquers all! It is greater than your expectation (hope) and pours its very essence into your faith! The TPT states it this way, *"Until then, there are three things that remain: Faith, hope, and love—yet love surpasses them all. So above all else, let love be the beautiful prize for which you run"* (1 Corinthians 13:13).

The Passion Translation emphasizes the depth and power of God's love, encouraging God's sons to embody this love in their daily lives. As in the scripture above, Ephesians 3:17 in TPT reads: "Then, by constantly using your faith, the life of Christ will be released deep inside you, and the resting place of His love will become the very source and root of your life." This verse highlights the preeminence of Christ's love as the foundation for spiritual growth and faith.

The recurring emphasis on love throughout Ephesians in TPT underscores its significance in fostering unity, spiritual maturity, and a deeper relationship with God. When faith is rooted in love, it becomes immovable, guiding your every thought, action, and decision.

After embracing your new Mindset of Faith, this should be your stance and how you live it out every day:

Ephesians 4:21-24: *"If you have really experienced the Anointed One and heard His truth, it will be seen in your life; for we know that the ultimate reality is embodied in Jesus! And He has taught you to let go of the lifestyle of the ancient man, the old self life, which was corrupted by sinful and deceitful desires that spring from delusions. Now it's time to be made new by every revelation that's been given to you. And to be transformed as you embrace the glorious Christ-within as your new life and live in union with Him! For God has recreated you all over again in His perfect righteousness, and you now belong to Him in the realm of true holiness"* (TPT).

This is LIFE-ALTERING! However, it is not a one-time event but a continual process of renewal, growth, and alignment with God's truth. As you walk forward in faith, empowered by love, you will discover that living in union with Christ is the definitive fulfillment of your purpose. This is the essence of the Mindset of Faith—one that is deeply rooted in God's love, continuously renewed by His Spirit, and fully aligned with His divine nature.

Now, as we move into the final chapter, we will bring together everything you have learned, setting the principles of faith, mindset, and love into a cohesive understanding that will guide you in living out your faith journey every day.

Your Work:

How can faith fueled by love operate in your life to fulfill your purpose?

_____
_____
_____
_____
_____
_____
_____
_____
_____
_____
_____
_____
_____
_____
_____
_____

NOTES

9

Putting it All Together

In this training manual, you have learned about the Mindset of Faith—its meaning; its foundation; and its purpose for you. Some key points about faith are:

- Faith is knowing the Character of God, and who He is.
- Faith brings an expectation and desire for positive outcomes.
- Faith IS NOW! It takes action to activate and to keep it working.
- Faith comes by Hearing, Speaking, and Acting on The Word of God.
- Faith goes beyond belief; Faith is what pleases God, not belief.
- Faith is a seed that is rooted in your heart and requires nourishment of God's Word to grow.

Understanding these fundamental aspects of faith, then guides you into having the power of bold faith. This *"dunamis"* **(divine enablement of God's supernatural, explosive power)** strength and ability causes active movement that initiates your words and actions to line up with God's Word.

Knowing this, you comprehend faith as a mindset; it transforms your perspective, enabling you to mature in faith, advancing you towards God's purpose for your life.

This led to the analysis of how the brain and the mind work together. You learned that:

- The brain is the physical, tangible, human organ that processes all bodily functions.

- The brain processes what our spiritual consciousness perceives.

- When the mind of man takes on the thoughts and ways of God, it causes you to have a Regenerated Mind.

- The regenerated mindset refers to the mind rewire process that takes place when the new life creation is imparted into you. It is the "new nature" (God's Divine Nature; His downloaded nature activated) in you that translates how you think, believe, and operate, and becomes your spiritual DNA.

- A new mindset involves intentional changes in your thought patterns and beliefs.

After getting an understanding of how your natural brain and spiritual mind work together, we then moved to discussing the difference between God-Consciousness and self-consciousness (their differences and how they align). This told you that:

- You are self-aware through your God-Consciousness, not self-consciousness.
- God-Consciousness transforms the mind so you live a life free of fear and full of faith.
- When your mind is saturated with God's Word, your faith becomes a natural response to life's challenges.
- To have God's Mind (His thoughts and way of doing things), you must be spiritually mature and have faith in what He has said (to you and about you).
- When God brings you into (His) Glory, you are to celebrate His Greatness and Excellence in you.
- The Mindset of Faith is having The Mind of God and putting it into action, giving you a higher degree of life.

Two of our foundational verse passages came from Hebrew 11:1 and 1 Corinthians 2:11-15.

Hebrews 11:1 states the end from the beginning: *Now faith brings our hopes into reality and becomes the foundation needed to acquire the things we long for. It is all the evidence required to prove what is still unseen.*

Once the definition for the word hope was established, the expounded version of Hebrews 11:1a became: *"Faith brings an expectation and desire from an optimistic state of mind for positive outcomes INTO reality".*

Our second passage read:

- **1 Corinthians 2:11-15 (TPT)** *After all, who can really see into a person's heart and know his hidden impulses except for that person's spirit? So, it is with God. His thoughts and secrets are only fully understood by His Spirit—The Spirit of God. For we did not receive the spirit of this world system but the Spirit of God, so that we might come to understand and experience all that grace has lavished upon us. And we articulate these realities with the words imparted to us by The Spirit and not with the words taught by human wisdom. We join together Spirit Revealed Truths with Spirit Revealed Words. Someone living on an entirely human level rejects the revelations of God's Spirit, for they make no sense to him. He can't understand the revelations of The Spirit because they are only discovered by the illumination of The Spirit. Those who live in The Spirit are able to carefully evaluate all things; and they are subject to the scrutiny of no one but God.*

What this taught was:

- You can only truly know God through His Spirit, not through your own human experiences. It is through understanding His Word that you gain the knowledge and revelation of who He truly is.
- When you are born again (become a son of God), you no longer live by the world's way of doing things. Instead, God gives you His Spirit (Holy Spirit), allowing you to

understand and experience the fullness of His grace. Through your transformed life, you align yourself with God's divine purpose. His Spirit enables you to walk in the richness of His love and the abundance of His blessings.

- When your mind is renewed, it changes your language to reflect what's within you creating what is outside of you. The words you speak are no longer shaped by worldly influences but are guided by the Spirit of God which alters everything concerning you. Spirit-revealed words that you speak into your atmosphere carry divine power, aligning with God's truth rather than human understanding. This shift allows you to speak life, faith, and purpose into every situation.

- Comprehension of God's Spirit and Spirit Revealed Truths is not possible through human intellectual capacity. The mind of man is not capable of this task without the Divine Nature (Spirit) of God operating to the highest degree in your life.

- When God's Spirit dwells in you and functions at its fullest and highest capacity, you have the aptitude to assess the value of all things pertaining to your life; and God is the one that will conduct the examination of "Himself" that lives in you; meaning, how much of Him are you allowing to shine through you.

To conclude the matter, you found out how love solidifies your faith mindset because:

- **Love is the Foundation of Faith** – Faith operates through love; without love, faith becomes empty and ineffective. Love is the driving force that strengthens and sustains a faith-filled life.

- **Love Transforms the Mindset** – When faith is rooted in love, it renews the mind, shaping thoughts, attitudes, and actions to align with God's truth rather than fear, doubt, or worldly influences.

- **Love Unites and Strengthens** – Love fosters unity with God and others, reinforcing the believer's confidence and trust in God's promises, leading to bold and unwavering faith.

- **Love Fuels Spiritual Growth** – As a son of God you embrace God-consciousness; love becomes the catalyst for deep spiritual transformation, ensuring faith matures beyond mere belief into a fully lived spiritual life.

- **Love Anchors Faith in God's Character** – Since God is love, a faith mindset grounded in love is firmly anchored in His unchanging nature, providing stability, endurance, and assurance in every season of life.

10

Declaring "IT IS SO" For You

And now that all these are established in your life:

I declare to you that you have the MINDSET OF FAITH. That God's DNA is evident in you, it empowers you to speak Spirit Revealed Words from Spirit Revealed Truths into your atmosphere, and causes every chain of bondage, every evil work, every dark place in your life broken and demolished!

I declare that the seed of faith that is planted in your heart continues to grow as you live out your relationship with Christ. That it elevates you from your infant stage of faith to your mature stage of faith that empowers every area of your being—spirit, soul, and body.

I declare that you have embraced your Sonship into the Body of Christ and that it has caused you to be awakened out of the sleep of your old mindset and spiritual complacency and has aroused your spirit being to the fullness of God's Glory Mindset. You live your life patterned after the Character of God and have adopted a new faith system that causes a disruption in your old way of thinking and doing things. And now you operate from a place of authority and rulership over everything in you and attached to you.

I declare your faith brings an expectation of your desires from an optimistic state of mind creating positive outcomes into reality. Faith is the foundation that your life is built upon, rooted in love. The Fruit of the Spirit are ever-present and working in your life, so that your inheritance in Christ is unlocked, and you are empowered to walk in total victory. Your life is full of purpose, prosperity, and divine success.

I declare that faith empowers you, moves you, translates you, opens you, motivates you, lives in you, sees you, embraces you, has authority in you, fixes everything pertaining to you, operates in you, has power in you, creates a new reality in you, inspires you, prompts you, enables you, has all certainty in you, rewards you, fulfills all purposes in you, stirs you, pulls you, provides in you, fastens to you, sparks you, and has its fullness in you!

I declare that you no longer imitate the ideas and opinions of the culture around you, but you enter into the spirit filled Culture of Christ, where your renewed mind is fixed on and submitted to God's Righteous Principles. Your regenerated mindset has imparted a new and divine life in you; you are a new creation with a totally new nature, which is God's DNA—His Downloaded Nature Activated in you!

I declare that you put your faith in action by practicing and developing your spiritual abilities activated as you live your daily life in Christ. You are no longer self-conscious, but you are God-Conscious which makes you self-aware through Him. You are ever-aware of His Presence, His Character, and His Will in you and for your life. Your God-Consciousness has transformed your mind and has created an atmosphere that ascends you above low-level thoughts of fear, doubt, and worldly distractions; you live in a higher realm of clarity, peace, and abundance.

YOU HAVE THE MINDSET OF FAITH IN JESUS NAME, AMEN!

Glossary

ALPHA and OMEGA – The Beginning and The End.

Being (State of) – To embody and live out God's Word to the extent that it becomes your identity, nature, and way of life.

Belief System – A collection of interconnected beliefs that determine how a person interprets reality and makes decisions. A belief system can be rooted in faith, culture, personal experiences, or societal norms, and it serves as a guiding force in one's life.

Belief – An acceptance that a statement is true or that something exists; A firm held opinion or conviction.

Brain – The central processing center of the human body (the physical being organ) that processes what your spiritual consciousness perceives. It is the command center for the nervous system that controls every process that regulates the body. It also operates separately from the spiritual mind.

Character of God – The unchanging nature and attributes of God, including His love, faithfulness, righteousness, mercy, and justice.

Core Belief – A deeply ingrained conviction that shapes a person's thoughts, emotions, and actions. Core beliefs are often formed through life experiences and influence how one perceives themselves, others, and God.

Divine Knowledge – Spiritual understanding and truth that comes directly from God. It surpasses human logic and intellect, providing insight into God's will, nature, and purpose through revelation, not just study. It is accessed through the Holy Spirit and the Word of God, giving God's sons understanding that leads to transformation and alignment with God's plan.

EL CHAY – The Living God.

ELOHIM – Creator of Everything.

El Roi – Sees All.

Faith – Complete trust or confidence in someone or something.

Fixed Mindset – The belief that abilities, intelligence, and talents are static and unchangeable. People with a fixed mindset often avoid challenges, fear failure, and believe that effort is futile if success isn't immediate. This type of mindset limits growth, especially in spiritual development, because it resists the renewing work of God in the mind.

Fruit of the Spirit – The evidence of God's Spirit at work in you; these include, love, joy, peace, patience, kindness, goodness, faithfulness, gentleness, and self-control; proof of a faith-filled life.

Glorification – The act of honoring, exalting, or praising someone or something to a high degree. In a biblical and spiritual context, it refers to the recognition of God's greatness and the process by which God's sons are elevated to a higher spiritual state, reflecting God's image and receiving His Glory.

Glory – As a noun: High renown/honor; Praise, worship and thanksgiving offered; often refers to the manifested presence and greatness of God. It can also be translated as glorification, which is a verb meaning the act of giving honor, praise, or exaltation to someone or something. Spiritually, glorification is the process of being elevated to a higher spiritual state and celebrating the excellence and greatness of God.

God-Consciousness – A mindset focused on God's presence, truth, and divine guidance, shaping thoughts and actions in alignment with His Will.

God's Divine Nature – The essence of who God is—perfect in love, righteousness, justice, holiness, and power. It is the nature imparted to God's sons through salvation, enabling them to reflect His character and operate in His likeness.

God's Grace – The unearned, undeserved favor and kindness of God extended toward humanity. Grace empowers His sons to live righteously and is the divine enablement to do what cannot be done by human effort alone.

God's Kingdom – (God as King, has dominion over all). The sovereign reign and rule of God as King over all creation—both in heaven and on earth. It is not only a physical realm but a spiritual reality where God's will, authority, and power are fully expressed. In God's Kingdom, He has absolute dominion over everything, and His principles of righteousness, peace, and joy govern the lives of His people. His sons are to live under His rule, align with His ways, and expand His Kingdom through faith and obedience.

Growth Mindset – The belief that skills, knowledge, and intelligence can be developed through dedication, learning, and effort. In spiritual terms, it reflects a heart and mind open to transformation through God's Word and Spirit, trusting that God can grow and mature His sons into who He has called them to be.

Holy Spirit – The third person of the Trinity; The Father (God), The Son (Jesus Christ), and The Holy Spirit- (God's Spirit) who indwells, empowers, comforts, and guides God's sons (regenerated spiritual beings) into all truth. He reveals the heart and mind of God and is the active presence of God in the life of God's sons.

Hope – A feeling of expectation and desire for a certain thing to happen; A feeling of trust.

Illumination of The Spirit – The process by which the Holy Spirit brings clarity, revelation, and spiritual understanding to God's sons, enabling them to comprehend God's Word beyond intellectual knowledge.

Incorruptible Seed – God's Word that becomes the seed of faith planted in you when you receive salvation that produces spiritual growth and transformation; this seed cannot decay, fade, or lose its power.

Infancy (Spiritual) Stage – The beginning phase of a believer's faith journey, marked by basic understanding, reliance on foundational teachings, and gradual growth in spiritual maturity.

Interdependence of the mind and brain – The dynamic and mutual relationship between the mind (our thoughts, beliefs, emotions, and spiritual awareness) and the brain (the physical organ that processes and stores information through neural activity).

Jehovah-Shammah – The Lord is there.

Maturity (Spiritual) Stage – A deeper level of faith where a believer operates in full understanding of God's truth, demonstrating spiritual wisdom, discernment, and Christlike character.

Mind – The intangible part of the human thought processes; the inner faculty of thought, reasoning, and belief where decisions are made and spiritual understanding is formed. It is the bridge between the soul and spirit, shaping how you perceive and respond to both God and the world. It processes information, forms attitudes, and influences actions.

Mindset of Faith – A mental and spiritual posture that fully trusts in God's Word, character, and assurances, regardless of circumstances. It is a renewed way of thinking that aligns with God's truth and enables God's sons to walk boldly in obedience, expectation, and spiritual authority.

Mindset – A set of attitudes, beliefs, and thought patterns that shape how a person sees themselves, others, and the world. It influences decisions, emotions, and responses to life's challenges. In faith, a godly mindset aligns with God's truth and operates from trust, not fear or doubt.

Neuroplasticity – The brain's ability to reorganize itself by forming new neural connections throughout life. It means the brain is adaptable and can change in response to new thoughts, experiences, and behaviors. Spiritually, this supports the truth that transformation is possible—especially through the renewing of the mind as taught in scripture.

New Faith System – Letting go of fear-based thinking and embracing a faith-centered perspective that empowers you to walk in purpose.

Reactive (Reaction) – Acting quickly and impulsively from emotion or habit, without spiritual discernment.

Regenerated Mind (The Mind Rewire Process) – Refers to the transformation that takes place when the human mind is renewed by God's Spirit and Word. Termed here as "The Mind Rewire Process," it is where old, worldly thought patterns are replaced with Spirit-led understanding. This renewal allows God's sons to think, believe, and act in alignment with God's will, enabling true spiritual maturity and the formation of a Mindset of Faith.

Regenerated Mindset – A complete shift in thought patterns and beliefs through the Holy Spirit, resulting in a faith-driven, God-centered perspective on life.

Renewed Mind / Renewal of the Mind – The transformation of the mind to align with God's truth and His will through the power of the Holy Spirit. It involves replacing old, worldly thoughts with Spirit-revealed truths and godly wisdom, and allows you to see, think, and act from a place of faith.

Responsive (Respond) – Making thoughtful, spirit-led decisions based on God's truth and a renewed mind.

Salvation – Preservation or deliverance from sin (harm, ruin or loss—death).

Self-Consciousness – A heightened awareness of oneself, especially in how one is perceived or judged by others or even oneself. It often involves insecurity, comparison, and an inward focus that can hinder spiritual growth and faith. In contrast to God-consciousness, it places emphasis on human limitations rather than divine possibilities.

Sonship- Son(s) of God -God's Sons & Daughters – The identity and inheritance of believers as children of God, walking in His authority, purpose, and divine relationship through faith in Christ. Our identity in God has no gender, it is asexual in the aspect of being without sex (gender).

Soul (of Man) – The mind, will, and emotions that shape thoughts, decisions, and feelings; it must be renewed to align with the Spirit of God.

Soul Salvation – The process of renewing the mind, will, and emotions through faith in Christ, aligning one's thoughts and actions with God's truth for transformation and wholeness.

Sovereignty – The supreme power and authority of God to rule over all creation. God's sovereignty means He is in complete control, nothing happens without His knowledge or permission, and His plans and purposes will always prevail.

Spirit of God – Another name for the Holy Spirit, representing God's presence, power, and personality at work in the earth and in His sons. It is God's Mind and His Way of doing things. The Spirit of God reveals truth, convicts, teaches, and empowers for godly living.

Spirit-Revealed Truths – Divine insights and understanding imparted by the Holy Spirit that go beyond intellectual knowledge. These truths are spiritually discerned and bring revelation of God's will, character, and Word, helping God's sons grow in faith and maturity.

Spirit-Revealed Words – Words spoken under the guidance and revelation of the Holy Spirit. They carry power, divine authority, and clarity beyond human reasoning, often bringing breakthrough, healing, and understanding.

System – A structured framework or set of principles that govern how something operates. In the context of faith and mindset, a system refers to the patterns, processes, and influences that shape one's thinking and behavior.

The Enlightened Knowledge of The Spirit – The deep, divine insight that comes from a Spirit-led understanding of God's Word and nature. It goes beyond facts and logic, producing wisdom, transformation, and intimacy with God.

The Rewire Process (of the Mind) – The intentional process of renewing and transforming thought patterns to align with God's truth. This involves replacing limiting or false beliefs with faith-based principles through meditation on scripture, prayer, and conscious effort to shift one's mindset.

True Spirituality – Living in alignment with God's will, walking in faith, and embodying the character of Christ (God).

Wisdom – In the biblical sense, it is the knowledge of God's divine plan, especially truths that were once hidden but are now revealed through His Spirit. It is the application of divine insight for righteous living, spiritual growth, and alignment with God's will.

Word Utterance – A spoken word, statement, or vocal sound. In the spiritual context, utterances—especially when Spirit-led—carry divine weight. They can release truth, activate faith, and create change when aligned with the will and Word of God.

References

Barrett, L. F. (2009). The future of psychology: Connecting mind to brain. Perspectives on Psychological Science, 4(4), 326–339. https://doi.org/10.1111/j.1745-6924.2009.01134.x.

Belief system. (2025). The Oxford Review. https://oxford-review.com/the-oxford-review-dei-diversity-equity-and-inclusion-dictionary/belief-systems-definition-and-explanation/.

Brain anatomy and how the brain works. (2025). Johns Hopkins Medicine. https://www.hopkinsmedicine.org/health/conditions-and-diseases/anatomy-of-the-brain.

ChatGPT. (2024, 2025). ChatGPT, an AI language model developed by OpenAI, was used as a writing assistant and research companion. It contributed by helping articulate spiritual and psychological concepts, rephrasing complex ideas, providing definitions, and assisting with structure and flow of content. It also supported the development of glossary terms and helped refine explanations to ensure clarity and accessibility for readers.

Created in His image. (1988). Source of Light Ministries International.

Google. (2024, 2025). Google was utilized as a general research tool to explore commonly accepted definitions, scriptural insights, psychological concepts, and scholarly articles related to faith, the mind, and neuroscience. It served as a gateway to reputable sources that helped inform and support the teaching points throughout the book.

Hill, N. (2020). Outwitting the Devil. Sound Wisdom.

Names of God. (n.d.). Love Worth Finding Ministries. https://www.lwf.org/names-of-god?gad_source=1&gclid=CjwKCAjwl6-3BhBWEiwApN6_khP6tJ2ilXT1M955JJkk94ETaZA92Dm_1L50HbKf7Q8klfAmFGDGWBoCLRgQAvD_BwE

National Institutes of Health (US); Biological Sciences Curriculum Study. (2007). Information about the brain. In NIH curriculum supplement series [Internet]. Bethesda, MD: National Institutes of Health (US). https://www.ncbi.nlm.nih.gov/books/NBK20367/

Rettig, T. (2017). Belief systems: What they are and how they affect you.

Watts, A. (2011). The wisdom of insecurity: A message for an age of anxiety. Vintage.

Biblical Translations

AMP – Amplified Bible. (2015). The Lockman Foundation. Published by Zondervan; The Amplified Bible, Classic Edition. (2024). Zondervan.

ESV – English Standard Version Bible. (2016). Crossway Bibles.

MSG – The Message Bible. (2002). Eugene H. Peterson. NavPress.

NASB – New American Standard Bible. (1995). The Lockman Foundation.

NIV – New International Version Bible. (2011). Biblica, Inc. Published by Zondervan.

NKJV – New King James Version Bible. (1982). Thomas Nelson.

NLT – New Living Translation Bible. (2015). Tyndale House Foundation.

TPT – The Passion Translation. (2020). Brian Simmons. BroadStreet Publishing.

NOTES

NOTES

NOTES

About the Author

Anita Newson (Page), also known as *AnitaN The Biz Coach*, is the founder and president of E-Merging Venture Enterprises, LLC. She is a dynamic TV Producer of *You Make A Difference TV* on the Zondra TV Network (and winner of the 2025 Best Micro Network); an International and Amazon Best-Selling Author, writing and branding coach, speaker, and business funding strategist with a passion for helping others give voice to their vision and a mouth to their mission. With over two decades of experience across communications, corporate training, career development, grant writing, and entrepreneurship, Anita equips individuals, nonprofits, and small businesses with the tools to grow, lead, and thrive.

Anita holds an Associate Degree in Journalism, a Bachelor of Arts in Communications, and a Master of Science in Communications. She has served as a certified CPR instructor, foster parent trainer, Ready to Work instructor, and Federal Funding Grantsmanship Scholar. Her background also includes leadership roles with the National Black Mastermind Charitable Organization and membership in The National Society of Leadership and Success.

A proud U.S. Army combat disabled veteran and dedicated mother of four sons and a grandson, Anita blends her faith, expertise, and life experience to inspire personal transformation, business growth, and spiritual renewal. Through her newest work, *Mindset of Faith*, she invites readers on a powerful journey to renew their minds, embrace God's truth, and live boldly in freedom and purpose.

Anita would LOVE to connect with you! Make sure to contact her or connect with her using the information below:

✉ **Connect with Anita:**
Email: AnitaNtheauthor@gmail.com

Schedule a Zoom Call: (Free Professional/Personal Consult)
https://bit.ly/4dBwOtz

Facebook: @AnitaNTheBizCoach
LinkedIn | Instagram | Alignable | YouTube | TikTok: @Anita Newson

www.ingramcontent.com/pod-product-compliance
Lightning Source LLC
Chambersburg PA
CBHW060535100426
42743CB00009B/1538